DEPRESSION

Jack Dominian

FONTANA/COLLINS

To Samaritans – the world over

First published by Fontana 1976

Copyright © Jack Dominian 1976

Made and printed in Great Britain by
William Collins Sons and Co. Ltd Glasgow

Contents

Preface

The first point which any publisher and author need to agree upon is the readership of a book. Who is the book written for? When this is clear, the contents can be arranged accordingly.

The difficulty facing an author who wants to write about depression is that the subject involves a wide variety of professional and non-professional groups as well as individuals interested in the subject. Thus depression concerns psychiatrists, doctors, medical students, social workers, nurses, clergy, the Samaritans, to whom this book is dedicated, counsellors in other fields and the public who, either as sufferers or as relatives and friends to sufferers, would like to understand the subject.

It is of course impossible to meet the detailed needs of all such groups. There are few specialized books devoted to the subject although all psychiatric textbooks cover it. Thus the specialist, who in this instance is the psychiatrist, has adequate resources. For the rest the available material is scant, although growing in recent years.

This book stems from my experience as a psychiatrist and therefore as one familiar with the professional world of medicine and the allied fields of psychology and the social sciences, and also from my contact with many of the non-professional groups of workers, particularly the Samaritans and marriage counsellors, who come to the assistance of those who need help with depression and its allied states.

It has been written in the first place as an introduction to the subject for all professional workers and as an aid to all non-professional counsellors but it should also be of use to anyone interested in depression and its treatment. Such an aim risks the danger of being on the one hand too technical and on the other of diluting the technical sections to a point at which they no longer do justice to the scientific work recorded. I have tried to avoid these twin dangers (with what success only the reader can judge) and have given extensive references to original studies throughout the book so that those interested can pursue some aspects further.

I am very grateful to my publishers for assisting with the editing to ensure that non-professional readers are not over-whelmed or bored by technicalities. And yet a minimum of specialized language is unavoidably retained. I wish to thank Professors R. E. Kendell and J. L. Gibbons for their criticism and advice, although I remain responsible for any deficiencies and errors in the final text. Last but certainly not least I wish to thank all those who have allowed their experiences to be included in the book.

Dr J. Dominian
June 1975

Acknowledgements

The author and publishers gratefully acknowledge the following for permission to quote from works in their copyright: the author and Michael Joseph Limited for the extracts from *Diary of a Mad Housewife* by Sue Kaufman; the author and The Hogarth Press Ltd for the extract from *Attachment and Loss*, Vol. 1 by Dr John Bowlby; the author and Methuen and Co. Ltd for the extract from *On Aggression* by Konrad Lorenz; the author and Tavistock Publications Ltd for the extract from *Bereavement* by Dr C. M. Parkes; the editor and the Lumen Vitae Press of Brussels for the extracts from *Death and Presence: The Psychology of Death and After-Life* edited by A. Godin; the translator and Penguin Books Ltd for the extracts from Dante's *Divine Comedy: I, Hell,* translated by Dorothy L. Sayers; the author and Constable and Co. Ltd for the 'Twenty Principles of the Samaritans' from *The Samaritans in the Seventies* by Chad Varah; the Society of Authors, on behalf of the Bernard Shaw estate for the extracts from *Selected Prose* by Bernard Shaw; William Collins Sons and Co. Ltd for the extract from *An Essay in Autobiography* by Boris Pasternak translated by Manya Harari.

Introduction to Depression

Depression is one of the commonest experiences known to mankind. However, the word is used for different conditions and a good deal of the difficulty in its description is the need to be clear which of its features is being described.

Depression refers first and foremost to mood. This may vary from feelings of slight sadness to utter misery and dejection. Secondly, it is used to bring together a variety of physical and psychological symptoms which together constitute a syndrome (the technical term for any collection of recognizable and repeatable symptoms). Finally, depression is used to indicate an illness which prevents the sufferer from functioning and requires active treatment to restore the body and mind to a state of health.

As a mood variation, it is often a short-lived, private and undisclosed experience even though those in close touch with the individual recognize it. When, as is not infrequent, it is a recurrent happening reaching the level of a syndrome, the sufferer is compelled to share his inner state with relatives, friends and acquaintances. What is shared are the symptoms, the manifestations: an exact description, or the nature of the condition itself, is usually outside the understanding of the sufferer and those close to him. Sooner or later, however, when the unease reaches the stage of illness, the majority – except those who are actively contemplating suicide – will seek some form of help. This can be from a non-medical or a medical source.

In the pre-scientific era a good deal of help was sought from those members of society who had the reputation of healers or wise men and women. Depending on the cultural setting, the depressed turned to priests, the elders, the witch doctor, or those known for their ability to understand and advise in these situations.

Nowadays many more people are turning to medicine and psychiatry. This book will cover both present-day knowledge and the current approach of medical science to depression.

Before pursuing a detailed analysis of the characteristics of those who seek relief from depression, some attention needs to be given to the process of registering and communicating the experience of depression itself.

In the next chapter various personal accounts will be given to illustrate the subject. Personal awareness and communication of the depressive state go through successive phases.

There are three situations which need to be considered in turn. First is the experience of the man or woman who feels depressed and the response of those intimately connected with them. Second is the alteration that occurs when this person goes to see a doctor, and third is the attitude of the doctor himself.

Science aims at clarity of description which leads to the setting up of suitable hypotheses and theories which are tested further by agreed criteria; the original formulations are upheld, modified or changed as knowledge develops. In scientific medicine the same principles apply. Thus the term depression as already indicated has a fairly clear meaning for doctors at the level of mood, syndrome and illness: although we shall see in subsequent chapters that there is a deceptive certainty in this language whose application is not without its difficulties. But how can sufferers know that they are reaching a level of depression which is beyond an appropriate norm to the situation?

The brief answer is that often they do not know, nor do they use such a term as depression to describe their state. Unless they are familiar with the condition through their circle of family, relatives and friends the usual path to discovery is through a lonely journey of personal exploration of recurring symptoms. These will usually be emotional as well as physical (they will be described in detail in the course of this book). People may suffer for a long time, sometimes their whole life, showing distressing symptoms, without being aware that these are manifestations of depression. In the past little could be done for such a person since the possibilities of treatment were limited. Nowadays the recognition of depression is increasingly important and will become even more so in the future, since the possibilities for the relief of the condition are continuously expanding.

Some people know that they are subject to recurrent moods of depression but are afraid to acknowledge the fact or do anything about it. Frequently they subject their relatives to unnecessary and, at times, appalling distress because of their failure to seek help. Fear is one of the reasons for this avoidance: the fear that confirmation of their state will somehow stamp them with a seal of inadequacy and failure. Whatever the reason, both the informed and the uninformed will eventually reach a breaking point and will be compelled to seek medical advice.

MEDICAL CONSULTATION

Irrespective of whether they have insight into their illness or not, a powerful fear lurking in the background is that they may be going 'mad'. Madness, with its sense of pending loss of control over self, loss of effective functioning and contact with the world around, and the imagined accompanying social degradation and humiliation, is an apparently invincible enemy which the patient dreads to face. Often it is felt that the doctor, and in particular the psychiatrist, will act like a judge and pronounce a sentence of doom, a powerful and irrevocable sentence which will destroy the last vestiges of the patient's respectability and integrity.

Although these feelings of helplessness and despair may emanate entirely from the patient's own mental state, they are frequently exacerbated by the attitude of a society which still approaches psychological disorder with fear and suspicion. When the reality of what is happening is finally explained it is often found to be less terrifying, and a large proportion of those who do seek help find it in varying degrees, although undoubtedly much energy is still consumed by fear of the unknown. As the doctor is also a member of society and therefore shares its conventions, his attitude and suggested treatment is bound to vary from doctor to doctor far more in this subject than in other areas of medicine.

THE MEDICAL ATTITUDE

Before the modern era of rapidly increasing understanding of depressive states many victims of depression displayed behaviour which was interpreted only in social and moral terms. The lack of energy and enthusiasm, attention, concentration and perseverance could all be conveniently put down to slackness, laziness, lack of moral fibre, irresponsibility or a host of similar explanations. The family and physician would agree on the 'diagnosis' and the victim would continue to suffer until spontaneous remission or complete exhaustion took over.

Nowadays, having heard the patient's account, the doctor will frequently be able to reach the correct diagnosis. The word diagnosis has a formal and off-putting air about it. What is the significance of such a diagnosis? Is it simply a label which pigeonholes someone into a convenient category? What happens when one is labelled a depressive?

The concept of depression considered as an illness leads one to suppose that, like appendicitis, once the diagnosis has been made the treatment should follow promptly and be as effective as appendicectomy.

The facts are rather different. The word depression approximates much closer to a word like pain. Everybody knows the experience of pain and knows equally that there are many types of pain. Just as there are stabbing, gnawing, sharp, colicky, surface, deep, persistent, intermittent, fleeting and severe pains so there are fleeting, persistent, deep, fluctuating moods of depression accompanied with or without anxiety, tension, agitation, with or without physical and intellectual symptoms.

In brief, depression at the level of a syndrome or illness is not a clear-cut and precise entity. Psychiatrists have argued – and are still arguing – about its nature and in later chapters some of the reasons for this debate will be given.

In the practical situation of the consulting-room neither

the doctor nor the psychiatrist will normally wish to confront the patient with an academic lecture about the subject. They will use the convenient term 'depression' to cover a marked change of mood, syndrome or an illness. All of these need sympathetic understanding and management, particularly the latter two.

These involve the patient in a serious deterioration of the physical and mental state which in turn require psychiatric intervention and treatment and secondly those less severe states which do not threaten life so immediately but which nevertheless lead to a significant debilitation and therefore call for relief.

TREATMENT

Basically treatment takes the form of tackling the depression with social, physical, psychological and spiritual means or a combination of these. These will be described in detail subsequently but at this stage it is important to state the obvious. Some of these means are not widely available — for example psychotherapy. Furthermore, doctors will undoubtely have their own biases regarding treatment, reflecting either their medical training or personal attitude. For example there will be those who incline to the use of physical means such as pills and electric shock therapy far more readily than psychotherapy and vice versa.

The indisputable fact remains, of course, that everybody can be offered pills (whether they are actually taken is another matter) but, unfortunately not everyone can be offered expert psychotherapy or social case work. Nevertheless the successful outcome of each and every depression depends on a sensitive and accurate matching of the needs of the individual and the help provided by the medical practitioner coupled with any other non-medical support. This in fact demands a constructive and trusting alliance between doctor and patient which, unlike other conditions, requires far more than an accurate diagnosis and appropriate treatment *made and given* by the doctor *to* the sufferer. It requires a patient and mutual exploration of sometimes more than one approach until a suitable combination of what is available and what is possible brings about the desired relief.

Some readers may notice that the word relief rather than cure has been used. This is deliberate and suggests a general answer to a question that is often raised. Cure means restoring to health, but is often associated with the notion of the once-for-all reversal of the noxious process. An appendicectomy for appendicitis is the accepted pattern of disease and treatment which implies that whatever has gone wrong will never happen again. Conditions which require surgical intervention for removal or repair approximate much more closely to this model of disease than medical ones which have a tendency to recur. Certainly depressive illness can be treated in such a way that all the symptoms disappear, there is a restoration to complete health and the condition need never reappear *but as it may well do so* no responsible doctor can talk of cure, if this implies the guarantee of a permanent safeguard against a recurrence. The most he can do is to reassure the patient about the outcome of a particular episode.

The likelihood of further recurrences depends on some factors which will be considered in detail in Chapter xix.

I The Experience of Depression

Depression is felt as an impoverishing sensation which extends and invades the outer world, gradually stripping it of meaning and significance. Shakespeare describes it aptly through Hamlet:

> I have of late, — but wherefore I know not — lost all my mirth, forgone all custom of exercises; and — indeed — it goes so heavily with my disposition that this goodly frame, the earth, seems to me a sterile promontory.

The description goes on to illustrate the marked contrast between the objective richness of nature and the subjective lack of appreciation of its beauty.

> This most excellent canopy the air, look you, this brave o'erhanging firmament, this majestical roof fretted with golden fire — why, it appeareth no other thing to me than a foul and pestilent congregation of vapours.

Inner and outer draining of effort reduces the meaning of being and of interpersonal relations to nought.

> What a piece of work is a man! How noble in reason! how infinite in faculties! in form and moving, how express and admirable! in action, how like an angel! in apprehension, how like a god! the beauty of the world! the paragon of animals! And yet, to me, what is this quintessence of dust? Man delights not me — no, nor woman neither.

Hamlet, Act II, Scene II

What Hamlet describes as the loss of mirth is an invasion of the personality by a disintegrating force with multiple psychological and physical characteristics subtly intertwined. This is how it is described by a forty year old housewife and mother of four children with long experience of recurrent episodes of depression:

There are certain basic things common to all my own periods of depression, irrespective of whether they are slight, moderate or severe. These are principally feelings of an acute sense of loss and growing diminishment, feelings of inexplicable sadness amounting to melancholy, and the awareness of being trapped and becoming increasingly powerless. This trapped feeling always leads to panic at the growing realization that I cannot by my own efforts either elevate my steadily sinking mood or shorten by one day the length of the attack.

Two things always happen very quickly. I forget that all previous episodes of depression have eventually ended and I lose all hope regarding the future. It is such an intensely here-and-now experience that I forget any good in the past – any memory of the past is coloured so strongly by the blackness and badness of the present. The same is true of the future – it can only be as bad as, or more likely, much worse than the present.

A kind of isolation sets in; a peculiar paralysis of mind and body in which you exist simply as a state of pure pain. The feeling that you have ceased to exist at all is only disproved by the intensity of the pain felt. Pain is the proof that you are still alive, if not kicking. It is not felt as a welcome discovery; some kind of proof of extinction would be preferable.

She then goes on to elaborate on a combination of physical manifestations and her emotional reaction to them which are euphemistically described as 'fringe effects'.

The fringe effects, the little added extras of depression, are almost too numerous to mention. The endless crying, intermittently day and night, and the misery impossible to describe of waking up already crying, with the grim realization that another day has arrived to get through somehow.

The day follows the night with its varying kinds of

insomnia; bearable some nights but not others. The night becomes a ghost that haunts in the way that fear, guilt and despair are magnified during the sleepless hours. On other nights there is just oblivion accompanied by the frustration of sleeping all night and waking up tired out and weary beyond belief.

The thought of having to do anything at all makes you realize just how weary you are. Things which have to be done, like washing and ironing, get put off because you cannot cope and they mount up until either you cease to care or else you panic.

Guilt comes in like the tide, and you readily accept the blame for every ill there is in the world. The guilt comes from within and one can become so morbidly reflective that a feeling of total badness takes over.

Having spent most of the day urging yourself to go out and do some necessary shopping, you manage it and get out – only to find that you don't know what you need and it doesn't matter anyway.

The symptoms really do seem endless – the cynical despair with which you receive the good things of life – such as sunshine – because they seem to be such a mockery.

There is a kind of irritability that cannot be controlled – the inability to get away from noise – and all noise sounds magnified to an unbearable degree. The reaction to noise or frustration is usually either helpless crying or uncontrolled anger. After an outburst of anger you get more depressed because it seems to confirm your own intensely felt feelings of badness, and the guilt of it all plunges you downwards in an endless spiral.

Physical lassitude can be combined with either mental apathy or mental agitation. Either you sit unable to cope, not caring any more, or you sit unable to cope and getting more and more stewed up about it, willing yourself to get up and get something done. Either way you reproach and blame yourself and get ready to fend off the reproaches, spoken or unspoken, of those with whom you have to live.

Complete loss of interest in former interests and pleasures

means a kind of restless, frustrated boredom. Nothing seems worthwhile any more, especially eating. Shopping and cooking become huge tasks beset with insurmountable problems. Trivial decisions have to be made, and you can't make one, and hours go by and panic sets in because you can't think and can't do anything.

This growing diminution of physical energy and personal awareness, surrounded by a mounting sensitivity and irritation, makes contact and communication with others difficult and, at times, impossible.

The weariness of it all makes colossal demands of the will to go on speaking to other people or even putting up with their presence.

You cease completely to care about your family and friends. No one can get through to you. You hate them for trying and hate them for not trying. You hate people for caring because you feel unlovable and you hate them for not caring because you want to be loved. Either way, you lose. The conflicts that opposing feelings like these bring are unbearable.

Similarly the people you come in contact with have effects which you cannot predict – and so you try to avoid them. Kindness and friendliness when encountered make you feel worse. A cheerful greeting from a shopkeeper makes you burst into floods of tears and is certainly not an incentive to go shopping.

The sight of other people being happy or efficient or busy makes you realize how useless you are and how helpless the situation you are in. Enormous feelings of resentment arise at having to meet other people's perfectly reasonable needs.

The breakdown of relationships with others intensifies feelings of isolation and uselessness as well as the creeping sense of personal dissolution which is described next.

You feel like a stranger to yourself and become detached in a curious way. Stepping outside, you can view yourself with a mixture of hatred and complete disinterest. Although your feelings for other people and for things go completely numb, at the same time you suffer an increasing awareness and consciousness, a kind of hypersensitivity to everything around you. Shape, colour and forms are experienced acutely with a corresponding increase in the pain felt. I can only think that it is painful because the frustration which is continual leads to you becoming aggressive And when you become aggressive then you get more depressed and so you continue along the vicious circle.

Any religious faith you had just vanishes and what takes its place is not just absence – which might possibly be bearable – but a frightening sense of despair, a kind of angry despair which is very self-destructive.

I lack the courage to die and I lack the courage to live. I do not want to do either. Neither do I want to exist in a state of indecision. The conflict this brings makes me feel very alone. The aloneness that one goes through in depression is a kind of anguish; there is no point in crying out because there are no words to express the confusion of feelings which are overwhelming and threatening to extinguish you. As this feeling of aloneness increases there comes a terrible dread that one day a kind of stupor will set in, and one day you will wake up unable to speak or move but still able to see and hear, and you will be completely at the mercy of others. And yet it would be a great relief to give up and let go, to cease completely from caring about anything.

Perhaps the loneliness of self-rejection coupled with the unending battle against self-destruction is the worst part of it all. It is a battle I have to fight again and again: each time I win, and I stay alive, there seems just a bit less will to live than there was the last time. It diminishes steadily, and the more you realize it the more frightening the whole thing becomes. You think you are going mad and know that you are very sane indeed; you think that 'it' has gone away – and it hasn't.

You begin to realize that the ice upon which you walk is very thin indeed, and getting thinner. Time seems to be running out as the inevitable comes nearer. And it is not just a question of it being inevitable – it appears the most desirable thing in the world, the thing most to be sought, and full of promises – the relief from the agony of despair; peace from all that threatens, or release from existing. And yet there is another side to it; for the feeling of being close to total disintegration is also part of the pain and the darkness of being depressed. It is a permanent dread – the dread of nothingness and the dread of the unknown. It is both to be welcomed and feared.

And so one avoids as long as possible bringing about what you most fear – perhaps it is better to try and battle against the destruction of oneself than bring it about in what would inevitably be a very final way.

I don't know the answer to the question which takes all my energy to live with. I do not know if there is an answer and quite a lot of the time I do not very much care.

To sum up, depression is being alone, in darkness, in pain, in despair – and being unable to move one way or the other.

The sense of confusion, the fear, the gradual shrinking of personal awareness to the point of threatened extinction is the voice of depression which comes through in the next brief account, also from a woman.

You get into a state when you don't care about anyone . . . You see life as a big black hole which is gradually swallowing you up. At first you feel sorry for yourself and then you even stop feeling sorry for yourself. You wonder what you have done. Why is it happening to you? You don't know what you have done. All you know is that the whirlpool you are in scares you stiff and you want to get out but you don't know how.

Both these accounts come from people with long and severe experiences of depression and for whom the enemy remains daunting and unconquerable. Others have made attempts to come to terms with the foe even though it is an uneasy truce.

When I am depressed, I feel black and threatened and seem to be apart from the world, watching it carrying on around me, aware of the happiness, excitement, irritation and anger going on, but it cannot touch me, in the same way that no one in it can help or understand me. It is like watching a play that has nothing to do with me, miserable but safe, as long as I am alone and not asked to play in it as well.

I become very aware of small things, my eyes seem to focus more and more on small things around me, a flower, a teapot or the steam rising from a saucepan. Light seems to shine on these things and the rest of the world gets darker, until I feel I must switch on the light. But I cannot read because the words seem to come and go from the pages.

I feel tired but I cannot sleep. I lie in bed thinking of something which suddenly becomes very exciting but if I try to get up and implement it, its whole point seems to evaporate like a mirage and I am left feeling betrayed by something – I am not sure what.

An ordinary day's routine which can at times go by without thought or apparent effort becomes as difficult as wading through treacle. A nagging pain seems to ache in some part of my body but when I try to locate it it moves to another part. I want to weep but have to give myself permission to do so. I don't want anyone to ask why I am weeping; I want them to know and accept it without trying to make me feel better.

I want to go to bed with a hot water bottle and a pot of tea and lots of cream cakes and a fire burning in the room and no one to disturb me.

When I first experienced these things and tried to force myself into a more acceptable frame of mind, I grew afraid which made the world get blacker and people further and further away until they were like small marionettes dancing up and down in front of me. When someone talked to me their face loomed large and distorted in front of my face.

Now I relax as these impressions come and the unhappiness I feel becomes almost cleansing. I try and enjoy, or rather experience everything instead of pushing it away because it is wrong and, when I return to the world and begin communicating again, I have more energy and real direction.

In these accounts, individuals are describing their own personal experience of depression. In such a description the inner world of pain, anguish, misery, confusion, is articulated with as much clarity as is possible. Frequently the sufferer has neither an extensive command of language nor a firm grasp of the bewildering flow of sensations and continues to suffer the physical and emotional manifestations without being able to make any sense of them. Even when the confusion can be put into words, it is coloured by the subjective interpretation of the victim's individual life history and personal situation. Consequently what is important to one patient may not be meaningful to the next person even though he too is also suffering from depression.

Given the range of individual accounts and the endless variations of personal meaning, psychiatrists have tried to reduce the mass of detail into groupings and categories which form the basis of diagnostic descriptions which will act as guidelines to the appropriate treatment.

Inevitably such a transformation from the individual and the subjective, to the collective and the objective produces a barrier between the language and meaning that the sufferer uses and the language and interpretation that the psychiatrist applies. Scientifically based medicine does precisely this, namely converts the patient's sensations and symptoms into diagnostic descriptions that have a cause and effect relationship.

In so far as psychiatry has followed the medical world, it has attempted to apply the same descriptive principles of classification. Unlike other branches of medicine, however, psychiatric disorders involve a patient's whole personality to such a degree that this copying of the older branches of medicine has been criticized and often patients leave the doctor's consulting-room feeling they have received a label and a prescription but little sense of being understood in their personal predicament.

Bridging the gap between subjective experiences and formal psychiatric classification is a constant challenge to the practice of good medicine in any of its branches but it is of particular importance in psychiatry.

The next chapter will give an outline of the type of descriptive categories which psychiatry uses.

II Types of Depression

The classification of depressive illnesses has provided psychiatry with one of its most controversial topics which has yet to be satisfactorily resolved. The issues are highly technical but essentially concentrate on the question whether there are different and distinctive types of depression or whether there is basically only one type with two broad distinctive groups of symptoms which form what have been technically called the endogenous or reactive (neurotic) poles. The problem can be roughly illustrated by taking a familiar physical characteristic such as height. The argument would then be whether there are two distinct and different groups of people, the tall and the short, with entirely different sets of features distinguishing them or whether height is a single characteristic with a wide range from those who are very tall to those who are very short with most people somewhere in between.

The history of this controversy has constituted a central part of British psychiatry for the past half century and it involves many of its leading figures. To the layman and the majority of medical practitioners the debate is unimportant. Yet there are important theoretical and practical implications, for example in the treatment of the condition, which perpetuate it.

The story begins with the father of modern psychiatry, namely Emil Kraepelin, who, with rare insight based on careful and intense clinical observation of patients, divided the mass of heterogeneous mental illnesses into two main categories, namely schizophrenias – or as he called them *dementia praecox* – and the manic depressive group. He continuously revised his classification and by 1913, in the eighth edition of his book, he was able to embrace all mood variations under the category of manic-depressive psychoses.[1] These mood variations involved slight and severe forms of depression and the question that soon began to be debated in Britain was whether they were distinct entities or not.

A few years later Sigmund Freud's work began to penetrate the psychiatric world and the word neurosis took on a distinctive meaning in relation to intrapersonal and psychic conflict. Was there a difference in depressive phenomena between those described as neurotic and those described as psychotic?

Psychiatry began to divide itself into two different traditions. The followers of Freud formed the psychoanalytic group who worked mainly in their own consulting-rooms using psychotherapeutic techniques and avoiding physical methods of treatment. The successors of Kraepelin continued to work primarily in mental hospitals and used the currently acceptable physical methods of treatment. These two groups began to take sides on the issue of depression. Those who favoured the psychodynamic or Freudian approach considered depression a form of neurosis, which was a reaction (hence the term reactive) to stress and did not need admission to a mental hospital, but responded to psychoanalytic treatment. The others considered depression a psychosis, a severe form of mental illness, which required admission to a mental hospital; while it might have been precipitated by stress factors this was not essential and the cause was not merely reactive to such stress but an integral part of the patient's make up.

The Maudsley Hospital, a leading psychiatric centre in London, took a prominent part in this controversy through the views of the various members of its staff but particularly of two of its professors. In 1926 Professor E. Mapother entered the controversy by a decisive answer in the negative. He did not believe that there were in fact two types of depression.

The distinction between what are called neuroses and psychoses has really grown out of practical difficulties, particularly as regards certification and asylum treatment. It has become customary to call these types and degrees of mental disorder which rarely call for such measures by the name of neuroses. I can find no other basis for the distinction; neither insight nor co-operation in treatment, nor susceptibility to psychotherapy will do.[2]

In other words the need to enter a mental hospital or not was not an adequate basis for differentiating the depressive illnesses.

The absence of any difference between endogenous and neurotic or reactive depression was further advanced by an outstanding study of 61 patients carried out by Dr A. Lewis, later also to become professor at the Maudsley Hospital.[3 4] Other psychiatrists who could not support the distinction were Dr D. Curran,[5] later to become professor of psychiatry at St George's Hospital, London, and Dr G. Garmany.[6] On the other hand the maintenance of a distinction was insisted on by Dr H. Yellowlees,[7] Dr R. D. Gillespie[8] and Dr C. H. Rogerson.[9]

The Second World War came and went and the controversy remained. The fifties introduced new forms of treatment in the form of antidepressants and the argument now continued along new lines, namely that the two groups of depression, the endogenous and the reactive (neurotic) required different forms of treatment.

Further major studies were produced in the sixties and seventies supported by advances in statistics and the use of computers. A number of the papers came from the Department of Psychological Medicine at the University of Newcastle-on-Tyne, containing fresh evidence to substantiate the distinction between the neurotic and endogenous varieties.[10 11 12]

On the other hand the traditional position adopted by workers at the Maudsley Hospital was confirmed by another major study carried out by Dr R. E. Kendell[13] and a later study involving American patients as well.[14] It was concluded that there was no evidence that could indicate two distinct types of depression, an endogenous and a neurotic variety.

One authority sums up the issue thus: 'The controversy about the nature of depression can be reduced to the question of whether it is to be regarded as a single illness with differing manifestations or as a number of illnesses with at least one common symptom, depression of affect.'[15] The distinction is fundamental and in fact throughout this controversy what has been at stake is the attempt to distinguish clear categories of illnesses so that the patient receives the benefit of distinctive treatment, precise understanding of outcome and, if possible, help with prevention.

At the time of writing the controversy remains unresolved, even if the protagonists are drawing closer. The beneficiary of this epic scientific debate will undoubtedly be the patient, whose interest is ultimately at stake.

ENDOGENOUS DEPRESSION

Despite the continuing argument, in practice depressions with two broadly different groups of manifestations are seen and, since there is some evidence that they respond differently to the available methods of treatment, they will be considered separately.

The endogenous or more severe type of depression is diagnosed according to the following criteria, which for convenience can be divided into psychological and physical.

Psychological Symptoms

(i) *Mood changes*. The principal manifestation in all depression is the change in mood. Mood describes the state of feelings, and in depression there is a shift towards sadness, misery, increasing gloominess, blackness, and finally utter despair. At some future date, advances in psychiatry will permit a correlation between this type of change and some easily assessed laboratory measurement which will confirm beyond doubt the change of mood. At present no such criterion exists and the accurate assessment of mood changes remains a skill, an art on the part of the doctor. Usually there is no difficulty in reaching the correct conclusion; occasionally there may be. The reason for this is that patients themselves may not feel this mood change clearly or they may be so afraid of acknowledging it that they go to great lengths to hide it from themselves and their doctor.

Sometimes the depressive mood component is missed because the patient may experience a lack of pleasure or enjoyment rather than an active and clear-cut sensation of misery. Indeed on rare occasions the deception between doctor and patient may be so complete that a very severely depressed person may in fact give the appearance of being utterly relaxed and smiling, a condition which has given rise to the term of the 'smiling depression', a state which, if missed, may have fatal consequences for the victim.

A common and frequently observed feature of severe depression is the variation in intensity. Depression is often – but not invariably – worse in the morning and begins to improve in the course of the day, becoming less evident towards the evening.

(ii) *Psychomotor Retardation and Agitation.* In the presence of such misery other features coincide with the mood. Thinking and purposeful activity become progressively less effective and ultimately cease altogether.

This gradual slowing up is noticed in the whole process of thinking. Forming an idea becomes difficult, and the effort required to concentrate or pay attention to what is happening more and more demanding. This reduction of interest involves both the familiar and the new. Newspapers, radio, television, books are gradually abandoned or, if pursued, become more and more difficult to follow or understand. The same happens with the familiar and the routine. Work that has been second nature appears incomprehensible or a labour of Herculean proportions. More and more time is spent achieving less and less, with many more mistakes than usual.

Anything new in the course of work is simply not tackled. At home the conversation of the members of the family is listened to but hardly registered and the replies become perfunctory and often unrelated to the point at issue. Speech becomes reduced to the bare minimum with, at times, monotonous repetition of particular phrases. Soon it will be noticed by the sufferers or their relatives that not only their span of attention and concentration is severely reduced but their memory is also failing.

The deterioration of memory has a most frightening impact and is undoubtedly one of the symptoms which threaten the patient with the notion of madness. We all rely on our memory for a sense of continuity of a meaningful life. Its deterioration, unlike the other symptoms, creates a personal fragmentation which is difficult to compensate.

For a while it helps to write notes and make shopping lists, but eventually the poor functioning becomes too obvious to hide from the immediate family or colleagues at work.

The diminution of mental functioning, characterized by reduction in levels of attention, concentration, alertness, initiative and persistence, is often paralleled by a similar decrease in physical activity. The person experiences an unexplained lassitude, tiredness which gradually becomes a lethargy showing itself in the desire to do less and less physically until, in the very severe instances, the patient simply sits or lies and stares into space.

This physical retardation is often camouflaged by the presence of agitation or anxiety or both. Agitation shows itself in an inability to settle down in a chair or on a bed. Instead the sufferer paces restlessly up and down, fidgets and wrings his hands with an agonized expression that betrays his acute state of distress. This state demands relief because it interferes with rest and food consumption and ultimately reduces the patient to a state of exhaustion.

In this state of utter apathy, restlessness, or a mixture of the two, consciousness narrows down to personal survival and the patient is unable to cope with anything else. Work, personal appearance, the needs of others, are all neglected. This indifference to life may finally take a self-destructive quality and suicide be actively contemplated.

(iii) *Loss of Self-Esteem*. In the presence of such devastating loss of mental and physical functional effectiveness there is inevitably a loss in self-confidence which easily becomes a loss of self-respect. Feelings of inferiority, inadequacy and ultimately uselessness amass and progress to a point where the sufferer is no longer rational.

(iv) *Delusions*. The feeling of self-depreciation now assumes an intensity that inhibits reason so that it can no longer provide a degree of reassurance. The delusions, which are irrational beliefs no longer open to the correction of reason or persuasion, assume the character of utter despair, hopelessness and self-reproach.

At this stage the victim interprets his condition as so extreme that he convinces himself that he has been abandoned, and justifiably so, by relatives, friends and God. All that is left is a contemptible wretch, a burden to family and friends, and deserving no better than to be left to die. This is the just punishment for some real or imaginary misdeed which becomes a vital secret. The secret may be the imaginary stealing of goods, misappropriation of funds, sexual misconduct, or an exaggeration of ordinary frailties.

These self-reproaching delusions may also be accompanied by the conviction that others are aware of all these crimes and are perpetually making references to them. Everybody seems to know of his wickedness, to be talking about him and avoiding his presence. It seems that nothing but the most severe punishment will expiate the crime. For religious believers this can mean the certainty of eternal damnation.

(v) *Hallucinations*. Hallucinations are sensory experiences in the absence of an appropriate stimulus. For example, a patient hears a voice when no one is there or sees something that is not present. Such hallucinatory voices carry messages of gloom and condemnation.

The delusions and hallucinations which the patient experiences usually derive from and fit in with his social, cultural and personal background. People with a strict sexual upbringing will experience fears about their sexual degradation, while others with over-conscientious standards will be concerned with violations of financial integrity, and citizens with many years of devoted public service will believe that their actions are responsible for the appalling state of the world.

It is, of course, vitally important to recognize the mistaken nature of these delusions and hallucinations and not to pursue what are almost invariably false trails.

(vi) *Disorientation.* In severe depressions the patient not only has these marked delusions but also ultimately loses all sense of time, place and personal identity so that the disorientation becomes complete and finally leads him to lose touch with his surroundings. In other cases where there is no disorientation, time seems to pass very slowly.

Physical Manifestations

(i) *Disturbance of Sleep.* All forms of sleep disturbance are common in depression. In the endogenous group one pattern is observed with sufficient frequency to have become recognized as one of the standard features of this illness. In this type of insomnia, the patient is able to go off to sleep with or without the assistance of a hypnotic but usually wakes up in the early hours of the morning, say at about 3, 4 or 5 o'clock, and cannot get back to sleep thereafter. This is a frequent but not invariable pattern.

(ii) *Loss of Engery.* Loss of sleep is eagerly seized upon as an explanation of the lassitude, tiredness and loss of energy which are almost invariably present. The fatigue may be partially accounted for by the loss of sleep but it is also part of a much wider reduction of physiological capacities. The fatigue cannot usually be accounted for by an equivalent degree of work and, indeed, patients are sometimes left with the paradox that the less they do the more weary they appear to be.

(iii) *Loss of Appetite.* The insomnia and loss of energy are often accompanied by a severe loss of appetite and sometimes the patient may lose a great deal of weight, which is wrongly interpreted as a sign of some form of lethal condition which only adds to the existing anxiety.

There is not only a loss of appetite but a loss of interest in food so that eating becomes a wearisome burden undertaken to pacify worried and nagging relatives. Food lacks taste and the most titillating morsels lose their significance even for the natural gourmet. Constipation may follow and can take a severe form.

(iv) *Loss of Sexual Drive.* Part of the general lowering of biological activity is also registered in the sexual drive which is often diminished and sometimes completely lost during the period of the illness. In women menstrual irregularities may also occur, such as irregular or heavy periods, or occasionally total cessation of menstruation.

This description of the severe or 'endogenous' type of depression will be familiar to the sufferers themselves, to their relatives and the medical profession, particularly the psychiatrist, who is inevitably called to help in this clinical situation. But to the overwhelming number of people who read this account and who have themselves experienced bouts of depression but have not consulted a doctor, it will appear as a strange and foreign description with which they will be unable to identify.

It is important to register the fact that this difference stems from the fact that doctors, and particularly psychiatrists, often have to concentrate their efforts on the severe manifestations of depression whereas the public at large usually experiences another type of depression which has variously been called 'reactive', 'neurotic', 'atypical' or 'less severe'.

REACTIVE DEPRESSION

The difference between the 'endogenous' and the 'reactive' types of depression is suggested by their names. The word 'endogenous' means literally growing from within and, as will be seen in the discussion in Chapter IV, the suggestion is that this type of depression is triggered off by factors which belong to the basic personality of the individual and are set in motion by biological changes in the organism obeying their own rules, which are not easily understood. Patients often ask in a puzzled way the reason for their illness when they cannot recognize any stressful event responsible for it.

On the other hand the word 'reactive' suggests a reaction to something that provokes a depressive response. Frequently the trigger action is related to some personal loss such as the death or departure of a relative or friend or sometimes a pet; material loss in the form of money, house or a precious possession; diminution in prestige by failure to achieve promotion, a desirable post, an academic advance or public recognition; or the loss can take the form of a rejection in personal relationships, such as marital breakdown or abandonment by a lover or close friends.

In all these instances the depressive reaction is assumed to be reasonable and related to the trauma that caused it in contradistinction to the endogenous form which appears to be unprovoked. While there is a lot of truth in this commonsense explanation, the facts do not bear it out. For example, trivial stress can usher in a very severe form of depression or none at all, and severe stress may produce little or no depressive reaction, while there are many people who are subject to recurrent episodes of fleeting, light depression without any obvious reason. Also those with the so-called reactive variety can deteriorate to the point of marked severity.

Most observers seem to agree that there are differences in the features of the less severe forms which can be observed in the basic symptoms, and in order to clarify what these are a comparison will be made between the principal manifestations of the endogenous and the reactive types of depression. These are placed side by side in Table 1 on page 38.

Psychological Symptoms

(i) *Mood.* As in the severe form so in the reactive variety the principal symptom is a change in mood towards either active deterioration into misery and gloom or a less pronounced loss of well-being and *joie de vivre*.

In the latter case when the intensity is less marked the mood fluctuates, usually improving in the company of well-

D   B

disposed relatives and friends, deteriorating when the person is alone or in the presence of another person with whom conflict exists.

The morning is often a bad time but there is no improvement in mood during the day and, if anything, the depression is worse in the evening when the person returns from work, or at week-ends.

(ii) *Psychomotor Retardation and Anxiety*. In the severe form thought and behaviour gradually suffer to the point where the life of the victim grinds to a halt. Attention, concentration, communication, memory, persistence, initiative, all deteriorate, processes that are accompanied by corresponding physical retardation.

In the reactive form the chief characteristic is the presence of marked anxiety which the patient is aware of, or soon becomes aware of, when it is pointed out.

Anxiety manifests itself, broadly speaking, in three groups of symptoms. The first involves the nervous and hormonal systems, which together are responsible for such common features as hot and cold flushes, sweating, palpitations, breathlessness, gastrointestinal disturbances such as dry mouth, nausea and diarrhoea, a knotted feeling in the abdomen and bladder disturbance in the form of frequency of micturition. The second pertains to feelings of fear. The fears can be wide-ranging such as anxiety before an interview, fear of situations such as the dark, crowds, aloneness, enclosed spaces (e.g. house, cinema, theatre, bus, areoplane), heights and, indeed, anything which is not familiar or obviously safe. Sometimes the anxiety is completely beyond the person's understanding; it lies in his unconscious and needs careful psychological probing. The third group consists of physical manifestations associated with persistent pain or discomfort in some part of the body, such as recurrent headaches, backache, painful periods or abdominal pain involving the intestines.

Such a high level of anxiety, which can express itself in one of many ways, is a frequent feature of the reactive type of depression, sometimes called the neurotic form. (Here the word neurosis bears one of its several meanings, namely a higher propensity towards anxiety.)

Here is an entry in the fictional diary of an American housewife whose husband suspects she is not well and from whom she is hiding her deteriorating condition.[16] It has a high degree of authenticity.

That was close. Close shave. Poor Jonathan. Touchy and disorganized he thinks I am. Jumpy and irritable. What I am is paranoid as a coot. What I am at times is so depressed I can't talk; so low I have to lock myself in the bathroom and run all the faucets to cover the sound of my crying. What I am at other times is so jazzed up with nerves I can't stand still and everything shakes, and I end up either having to take a pill or a quick sneaky shot of vodka – it depends which is available. What I am is suddenly afraid of most everything you could name. I will name a few I am afraid of

> Elevators
> Subways
> Bridges
> Tunnels
> High places
> Low places
> Tightly enclosed spaces
> Boats
> Cars
> Planes
> Trains
> Crowds
> Deserted parks
> Dentists
> Bees
> Spiders
> Fuzzy moths
> Cockroaches
> Teenage groups
> Muggers
> Rapists
> Sharks

> Fires
> Tidal waves
> Fatal diseases – every one known to man

The list could go on, but I can't.

The psychological features of defective attention, concentration and memory present in the severe form may also be present in this type but they are usually not so severe and, indeed, the person may be able to behave outwardly as if there was nothing wrong with him which at times makes his inner suffering a lonely affair, very hard to communicate to others or even to be believed.

There is rarely a physical slowing up, but tiredness is often present and the features of anxiety just outlined play a prominent role in the clinical picture.

(iii) *Loss of Self-esteem.* The severely depressed patient feels worthless and is finally convinced that within him are to be found all the possible reasons for his undoing and his present state of hopeless despair. His or her imagined badness is in fact intimately related to the depressive process and when the delusions lift all the excessive self-accusation and criticism will also disappear, leaving the normal personality intact.

The reactive depressive state is not associated with such excessive self-accusations. Rather it is often found in people with above average anxiety levels and marked variations in personality characteristics, to which is attached another of the several meanings of the word neurotic. Here the word neurotic is being used in the sense given it by dynamic schools of psychology which are concerned to describe defects and conflicts in the personality in terms of intra- and inter-personal relationships. These will be examined further in Chapter V. In the reactive type of depression such traits as lack of confidence, an excessive sense of guilt, a horror of hurting others, or incurring their displeasure, are primarily responsible for the maintenance of the anxiety, tension and associated depression.

Although medicine can suppress the symptoms of anxiety

and depression, it cannot by itself eliminate deep-seated weaknesses in the personality which may subsequently trigger off yet another depressive episode.

Thus, the sense of inferiority, shyness or inadequacy, the lack of confidence, the inability to fend for oneself, express aggression, act assertively, cope with criticism, refute rejection, feel wanted and appreciated or, indeed, of any significance whatsoever – some of the common traits found in the personality of those suffering from reactive depression – are not produced by the depression nor do they disappear when the depression abates and in that sense the individual personal problem which confronted the patient before continues to do so afterwards.

With anxiety there is often a much higher level of irritation expressing itself in irritable behaviour, unexpected and unwarranted flare-ups and, at times, persistent and overt aggression, features which are not conspicuous in the severe type of depression.

(iv) and (v) *Delusions and Hallucinations*. Delusions and hallucinations, often conspicuous in the severe form, are rarely found in the reactive type.

Physical Manifestations

(i) *Sleep Disturbance*. Sleep disturbances are also very common in reactive depression. The pattern, however, tends on the whole to be different. The most conspicuous difficulty is the inability to go off to sleep. People tend to go to bed late – midnight or even later – because they know that they will not succeed in falling asleep much earlier. Sometimes they may still be tossing around at 1, 2 or 3 a.m. before they go off and even then they will still wake up at frequent intervals. Nightmares are not uncommon and although the person wakes up at the normal time he doesn't feel refreshed. Occasionally there is a tendency to fall asleep for long periods during the day.

(ii) *Loss of Energy*. Fatigue is common, and once again it does not correlate with the amount of energy expended during the day.

TABLE I

Characteristics of Depression

Psychological	Endogenous	Reactive
Mood	A shift towards depression is marked, continuous and usually worse in the morning.	The mood is less severely depressed, fluctuates and gets worse, if at all, in the evening and when alone.
Psychomotor Retardation	Is marked and expresses itself by a general slowing up in thinking and activity.	Not marked, if at all.
Agitation Anxiety Irritation	Agitation is usually present.	Anxiety and irritability are the principal characteristics. Fears are commonly present.
Feelings of inferiority, uselessness and hopelessness	Markedly present but disappear with the lifting of the depression.	Not so pronounced but often other variations in the personality present.
Delusions of self-reproach and guilt.	May be marked.	Usually not present.
Hallucinations	May be present.	Absent.
Physical Insomnia	Marked, characterized by early morning waking.	Marked, characterized by difficulty in going off to sleep and further interruptions.
Appetite and weight	Severely affected.	Usually little change.
Libido	Can be lost completely or partially.	Usually little change.
Energy	Markedly reduced.	Variably reduced.
Bodily pain	Present – clears up with lifting of depression.	Present – may clear up or persist.

(iii) *Loss of Appetite*. This is not at all common or characteristic, nor is there an accompanying loss of weight, but the feeling of persistent nausea may in fact prevent the normal consumption of food, particularly first thing in the morning when the person finds it very difficult to eat or keep anything down.

(iv) *Loss of Sexual Drive*. This is usually not present but the markedly anxious female may have some menstrual irregularities.

These distinctions made between the two forms of depression, although found frequently, are not always reliable and ultimately it is the assessment of the total clinical picture which guides the practitioner. The clinical picture may be unambiguous but not infrequently there are many overlapping features. This has been one of the main reasons for the continuing dispute about the complete separation of the categories.

DEPRESSION IN OLD AGE

Depression is far more common in the second half of life even though it can strike at all ages. Part of the success story of psychiatry in the last twenty years is the increasing identification of depression in the elderly and the considerable success achieved in the use of modern treatment.

The elderly depressed patient often presents the picture of severe depression with marked delusions which take a bizarre form of utter nihilism. Such a man or woman believes that their inner world is rotting and that their brain, bowel and heart have ceased functioning. Their agitation is usually marked and the deterioration in their mental functioning can give a mistaken picture of senility and insanity. Correct diagnosis and appropriate treatment produce a most rewarding clearance of the symptoms and restore the individuals to their previous state of health.

Notes

1. Kraepelin, E., (1913), *Manic-Depressive Insanity and Paranoia,* Trans. Barclay, R. M. 8th Ed. Edinburgh
2. Mapother, E., (1926), *British Medical Journal* II 872
3. Lewis, A. J., (1934), 'Melancholia: a clinical survey of depressive states', *Journal of Mental Science,* 80277 80, 277
4. Lewis, A. J., (1936), 'Melancholia: a prognostic study and case material', *Journal of Mental Science,* 82, 488
5. Curran, D., (1937), 'The differentiation of neuroses and manic-depressive psychosis', *Journal of Mental Science,* 83, 156
6. Garmany, G., (1958), 'Depressive states, their aetiology and treatment', *British Medical Journal* II, 341
7. Yellowlees, H., (1932), *Clinical Lectures on Psychological Medicine,* pp. 203-8 London
8. Gillespie, R. D., (1929), 'The clinical differentiation of types of depression', *Guy's Hospital Rep.* 79
9. Rogerson, C. H., (1940), 'The differentiation of neuroses and psychoses with special reference to states of depression and anxiety', *Journal of Mental Science* 86, 632-44
10. Kiloh, L. G., Garside, R. F., (1963), 'The independence of neurotic depression and endogenous depression', *British Journal of Psychiatry,* 109, 41
11. Carney, M. W. P., Roth, M., Garside, R. F., (1965), 'The diagnosis of depressive syndromes, and the prediction of ECT response', *British Journal of Psychiatry,* 111, 659
12. Kiloh, L. G., Andrews, G., Neilson, M., Bianchi, G. N., (1972), 'The relationship of the syndromes called endogenous and neurotic depression', *British Journal of Psychiatry,* 121, 183
13. Kendell, R. E., (1968), *The Classification of Depressive Illness,* Maudsley Monograph 18, London, Oxford
14. Kendell, R. E., Gourlay, J., (1970), 'The Clinical distinction between psychotic and neurotic depression', *British Journal of Psychiatry,* 117, 257
15. Mowbray, R. M., (1972), *The classification of depression in Depressive Illness,* Charles C. Thomas, Springfield, Illinois
16. Kaufman, S., (1968), *Diary of a Mad Housewife,* Michael Joseph, Ltd., London, pp. 8-9

III Mania

The principal feature of depression is a change of mood in
a direction away from what is normally experienced as com-
fortable and acceptable towards fluctuating or persistent
misery, sadness, gloom or apathy. This change in mood can
take one of two opposite directions, moving either towards
depression or towards euphoria, the latter being known
technically as mania, or hypomania, depending on the severity of the change.

Mania can occur by itself. But it is not as precise an
entity as depression. The manic patient may change rapidly
into a mood of depression and quick changes from one state
to another are far more common than in patients who are
subject to depressive illnesses alone.

Here is the account of one patient who gives a succinct
description of the condition which psychiatrists have labelled
manic-depressive psychosis:

> A depression period starts with a feeling of general
> tiredness which does not respond favourably to resting
> or sleeping. Within a few days, a bitter taste develops in
> my mouth and I lose my appetite. At night I have diffi-
> culty in sleeping due to my feet being very hot, even
> with no bedclothes on them.
>
> Within a week or ten days, an intense feeling of de-
> pression sets in creating the impression that I am quite
> incapable of doing my job – unable to drive my car and, in
> fact, afraid to do anything involving any skill or respon-
> sibility.
>
> This deepens my feeling of depression and soon brings
> me to contemplating suicide.
>
> These depression periods last from one to four months
> and stop within a few days, for what reason I do not
> know.
>
> At the end of a depression I am, as far as I can judge,

normal for a few days, following which I enter a period of elation. This state lasts for about four to five months during which I feel on top of the world; I volunteer to take on far more work than is humanly possible and spend a lot more money than I can afford. I am pleased to meet people and particularly to make new friends.

Unfortunately my inflated plans are quite impossible to achieve and my very failure seems to be one of the factors which starts another period of depression.

In this personal account the cycles of depression and elation seem to follow each other, beginning and ending for no obvious reason. An explanation for this may be found in changes within the brain. Our knowledge of these changes will be considered later; in the meantime the state of mania needs further description.

The mood of the patient is markedly euphoric, being at a level of elation well beyond the normal reaction to exciting news or events. Sometimes the euphoria may indeed be prompted by some unexpected happiness but usually there is no obvious trigger. The person begins to experience and to express a general feeling of uplift. Life becomes far more enjoyable and exciting. Worries, uncertainty and doubts rapidly recede. Self-confidence and ebullience appear to be the chief characteristics of the victim's behaviour.

This overflowing effervescence tends to be superficial and shallow and mixed with it is an increased tendency towards irritability and irascible outbursts. So long as the bonhomie is endorsed by others there is no evidence of stress but, if challenged, the hypomanic individual has no reserves with which to back his euphoric ideas and plans and so falls back on frivolous and petty argument ending in incoherence.

Accompanying the euphoric mood is a lack of tiredness and an apparently inexhaustible supply of energy. Sleep is needed less and less and the person seems to be able to survive prolonged sessions of activity without feeling any ill consequences. This excessive energy, coupled with euphoria, is often associated with an overstimulation of the intellect. Increasingly elaborate, grandiose and exaggerated ideas and plans are put forward. New businesses and the setting up of companies are planned, previously intractable problems are solved at a stroke and no criticism of the proposed solutions is tolerated; household chores of long standing are treated as mere trivialities which should be completed in a jiffy.

The accompanying self-confidence and gregariousness lead to unprecedented social activity in which acquaintances, friends and relatives are treated to noisy displays of the person's elevated mood. The frequency of the parties, the lateness of their conclusion, the drink consumed, all point to the phoney character of what is happening. Unfortunately, the person's euphoric state of mind may lead him to spend large sums of money which either he doesn't have or, when he has them, are spent carelessly on trivia. The hypomanic patient is also liable to be exploited by the unscrupulous who see and seize the opportunity to gain by the illness.

The elevated mood and increased energy are also accompanied by an increase in the sexual drive, leading to behaviour that may be personally damaging to the patient or to others. The hypomanic woman gives the appearance of being a nymphomaniac. The increased sexual desire may lead to a loss of normal social and moral control leading to indiscriminate sexual intercourse with the spouse and/or others. There is not only a change in personal standards but a deterioration of judgment and caution so that contraceptive measures are unlikely to be taken and the risks of an unwanted pregnancy are high.

The man is similarly subject to an increase in sexual desire and may also appear to be behaving in a promiscuous and irresponsible way. The family recognizes all this as foreign and out of character but at the height of the attack the sufferer is not likely to be influenced by reasoning or advice.

The principal feature and difficulty of assisting a person in this state is the fact that the elation is so gratifying and pleasurable that, unlike the depressive counterpart, the patients do not see themselves as suffering from an illness, have no insight into their condition and have no desire to change. During this state they are in danger of losing large sums of money, alienating friends, workmates or business associates, becoming involved in sexual misadventures, undertaking commitments which they cannot discharge and endangering their livelihood.

The family and relatives are driven to distraction in this situation particularly when the illness is occurring for the first time and they are unfamiliar with its characteristic features. If it recurs, steps can be taken early on to intervene medically so that the damage is reduced.

Inevitably if mania persists it needs medical care. The accumulated expenditure of energy, the absence of sleep, which is often a prominent feature, and lack of nourishment produce progressive fatigue and deterioration of normal behaviour, leading to ultimate exhaustion needing hospitalization. If the patient recognizes the need for help at an early stage, hospitalization may be avoided by the appropriate use of medication.

MANIC ILLNESS

What has been described so far is a state of euphoria which has not developed into a full blown manic illness. When it does so the patient reaches the same state of severe psychosis as the depressed patient, but shows a completely different set of symptoms.

The mood is now jubilant and patients may entertain both delusions and hallucinations. The delusions may concern identity; for instance, they may consider themselves to be Christ-like super people with remarkable minds possessing the clues and answers to complex problems, or the key to the solution of world problems. They may be convinced that their ideas about home, work or people are fantastically important and they will not take no for an answer, even if their conversation is disjointed, their reasoning faulty and inconsequential. They believe themselves to be some sort of Messiah with a message to deliver. Sometimes their delusions are accompanied by auditory hallucinations in which they hear voices confirming or urging them on to persevere with their plans. Occasionally the hallucinations are visual and they are likely to describe visions which are vivid, colourful and full of significance. The delusions and hallucinations occur in an overactive, agitated person whose lack of sleep, increasing activity and boundless energy ultimately cause his speech to become incoherent and his actions disjointed and meaningless.

In these circumstances hospitalization, with adequate sedation, is imperative, even though there will be continuous protestations that they never felt better and that the person who needs treatment is everybody except themselves.

MANIC-DEPRESSIVE PSYCHOSIS

In the preceding chapter various forms of depression have been described and in this one the opposite end of the mood scale, hypomania or mania, has also been described. Most commonly the patient is subject to depressive attacks only, rarely only to recurrent attacks of mania. Some patients suffer the one followed closely by the other. When both extremes of mood occur separately or in succession, the description given is that of manic-depressive psychosis or, as the French call it, *folie circulaire.*

Manic-depressive psychosis is the term that could be applied to the patient whose case is reported on page 41. Sometimes the manic phase follows the depression. At other times the depression follows the excitation and, in rare instances, there may be a succession of intense swings of mood reaching illness intensity.

CYCLOTHYMIC PERSONALITY

At a less intense level, however, many more people experience mood swings. These affect their inner life and their interpersonal relationships.

Where the swing is towards depression, a wide range of features is exhibited and these need to be understood by the sufferer and those close to him or her if relationships are not to suffer.

In the depressed phase all activity slows down, the range of interests diminishes and the person withdraws into himself. He or she is not in a mood to talk, tends to be irritable, finds fault easily, over-reacts to criticism, is unsure of his or her judgment, and feels lethargic. Household chores are left undone, decisions are delayed, temper is short. In this state other people become unimportant. Their needs are ignored, their points of view dismissed, their legitimate claims flouted. Such a state is of course a downswing in the mood cycle. The avoidance of people and social activities, the withdrawal from close personal relationships – perhaps into solitary drinking – becomes a familiar and predictable process lasting days, weeks or even months.

It is essential that others recognize and understand it, for if the phase persists for more than a short period, such a person makes himself extremely unpopular. He or she is considered to be bitchy, bloody-minded, lazy, cold, indifferent, difficult, explosive – a reputation the person finds hard to refute or comprehend. In fact the victim feels low, cut off, guilty and, at times, frantic on account of feelings of isolation that he may or may not understand. Indicted by an uncomprehending outside world, self-condemned by conscience and the observable fact that so much is being neglected, the depressive phase carries with it an endless struggle for mere survival.

In such circumstances the upward swing is welcomed. Normality returns for a while. The features relax, communication is re-established, civilized conduct restored. The long-overdue housework, planning, decision making are all done and ambitious plans are laid for the future. Redecoration and spring-cleaning are planned; letters, visits, contacts are all projected, but little gets off the ground in time to avoid the next descent into a new mood.

The false hopes that were raised, the inability to fulfil promises to oneself or to others, make life not only unpredictable but slowly erode the basis of trust in oneself. When others criticize they are attacking an already demoralized self. Unless the nature of the mood swings is grasped and some acceptable way is found of conducting day-to-day life and accounting for its unpredictability, there is a danger of plunging into deep personal despair and of earning a reputation for permanent unreliability. Not only does the individual need to grasp his own emotional fluidity but, even more important, those in intimate contact with him have to understand the nature of these fluctuations if they are to make sense of their unpredictability and avoid inflicting the inevitable moral censures which such conduct normally elicits.

Less intense mood swings occur in most of us. They generate our optimistic and pessimistic attitudes to life and affect the inner world of hope and despair which influences so much of our basic living.

IV   The Significance
and Meaning of Mood
1: Genetic and Biochemical Factors

HISTORICAL

In the previous two chapters descriptions were given of various states of mood disturbances, emphasizing that the essence of depression and/or its opposite mania is a disturbance of mood. By mood is meant a state of feeling, with variable degrees of stability or fluctuation, principally concerned with sadness and grief, joy and pleasure, apprehension and fear.

An awareness of such mental states goes back to the fourth century BC and Melancholia was one of the four forms of madness recognized by Hippocrates and the school of Cos in Greece. Some five hundred years later, in the second century AD, the Cappadocian physician Aretaeus offered a description which includes many of the features that we would recognize in depression today.

> Those affected with melancholy are not every one of them affected according to one particular form; they are either suspicious of poisoning or flee to the desert from misanthropy, or turn superstitious, or contract a hatred of life. If at any time a relaxation takes place, in most cases hilarity supervenes ... the patients are dull or stern, dejected or unreasonably torpid, without any manifest cause; they also become peevish, dispirited, sleepless, and start up from a disturbed sleep. Unreasonable fear also seizes them, if the disease tends to increase ... they complain of life and desire to die.

The salient features of the lowering of mood are already observed and so is the association between depression and elation as well as the desire to die and the intimate link with suicide.

From the second century to the sixteenth no major advances were made but between the sixteenth and eighteenth centuries there were several accounts of depression which picked up and reiterated Areteaus's description.

The nineteenth century saw the breakthrough in description and classification which ushered in the modern era of psychiatry. Essentially, this expansion took place along two fronts, one emanating from the works of German and French psychiatrists, the other from Vienna and Sigmund Freud.

The background to this improved classification was the increasing establishment, towards the end of the eighteenth century, of asylums for the care of the insane. Here the mentally ill could be observed more carefully and their cases followed over a longer period of time. As a result of these detailed observations, descriptions began to emerge which were increasingly more accurate.

In the 1850s the French psychiatrists Baillarger[1] described *Folie à double forme* and Falret[2] *Folie circulaire,* both describing clearly the mood swings of depression and mania. From the German university clinics there emerged a further refinement of the classification of insanity into those conditions that involved predominantly feelings and emotions from which recovery was possible, and on the other hand those that involved both emotional and thinking functions from which there was no recovery.

The works of Griesenger and Kalbaum finally led to that of E. Kraepelin who was able to divide mental illnesses into two broad categories, namely *dementia praecox* – later to be called schizophrenia, and the manic depressive psychoses. The great English psychiatrist, Maudsley (after whom the hospital and institute of psychiatry in London was named), also divided insanity into affective disturbance and ideational. The word affect is used to describe a mental disposition related to feelings, and the manic depressive illnesses, which form a prominent part of affective disorders, became an important element in the interest and research of the Maudsley Hospital which, under the leadership of Professor E. Mapother and A. J. Lewis, contributed much to the present understanding of the depressive conditions.

The distinction between manic depressive illnesses and *dementia praecox* or schizophrenia meant that patients' symptoms could be used to place the sufferer in one category or another, even though in practice there was – and still is – an admixture of symptoms, particularly in the opening phase of the illness.

This separation remains to this very day entirely dependent on clinical features with no precise laboratory means of verification. In this sense psychiatry is a branch of medicine in which the art of accurate evaluation of symptoms continues to be supremely important; hence the likelihood of disagreement amongst psychiatrists about the diagnosis particularly at the early stage, or if the development of the illness is not typical.

Nevertheless from the First World War onwards it became possible to classify depressive and manic illnesses with increasing certainty, and various subdivisions within the broad division of affective disorders were further described.

There followed in Britain – but elsewhere as well – the debate already described regarding the single or multiple types of depression. This debate is not concluded yet, but in the meantime two other major developments have been proceeding concurrently. The first is the exploration into the causes of depression, divided in turn into physical and psychological factors and secondly its treatment. The (dynamic) psychological explanation deserves the next chapter to itself, and treatment will also be considered in detail later. This chapter will now conclude by examining the important information, derived from genetic and biochemical studies, about depressive illnesses.

GENETIC FACTORS

Once psychiatrists learned to classify individual patients into different categories of depressive illness, they were able also to investigate the possible contributions of genetic factors in this illness.

The influence of genetic factors on an individual's behaviour is usually considered in what is known as the 'nature' versus 'nurture' contribution towards the development of the personality. By 'nature' is meant the inclusion of the elements which are present at the inception of life, at the moment of fertilization of the ovum by the sperm. From this fertilized single cell the foetus grows and this growth depends on the structure of the zygote, one half of which is derived from each parent. Thus through heredity the germ cells of the parents influence the development of the child. The units of heredity are the genes and their instrument of transmission, the chromosomes. Psychological illness may result through the dominant or recessive influence of a single gene or the accumulated influence of many genes.

In addition to the genetic inheritance, the foetus is also subject to any damaging influences which reach it via the mother. The thalidomide tragedy shows the danger of drugs which interfere with normal growth. Disease can also interfere with normal growth. One of the most familiar examples is the damage caused by German measles (rubella).

So far the development of the child is influenced by the genetic and environmental factors obtaining prior to its birth. After birth the child is subjected to direct interpersonal experiences between itself and its parents, first the mother, later the father, and soon a whole host of other people – brothers, sisters, relatives, teachers, friends. Here is a collection of influences which come under the category of 'nurture', or the impact of the environment.

The adult personality is the composite, complex product of these two contributions, the genetic-constitutional, or 'nature' and the environmental, interpersonal, or 'nurture'. As soon as the classification of the depressive illnesses became sufficiently clear to enable us to categorize patients confidently into one of various varieties there emerged the possibility of studying the relative importance of genetic-constitutional versus environmental factors.

Results of several studies have shown that there is indeed a contribution to the illness which is genetically inherited but its nature is far from being absolutely clear. It is known, for example, that the risk of having a similar type of affective illness, or the morbidity risk, is 10-15 per cent in the first degree relatives of patients who have had such an illness.[3] This is well above the average rate for the population, as a whole. However, it can be argued that this is accounted for by cultural transmission.[4]

One way by which the distinction between cultural or environmental factors and genetic inheritance can be sharpened is through the study of the health and disease characteristics of twins. As is well known, there are two forms of twins. The first is called identical or monozygotic (MZ) and comes from a single zygote, a single egg cell or ovum being fertilized by a single sperm. Identical twins represent two copies of a single individual and their inherited characteristics are wholly identical. Non-identical or two-egg twins, called dizygotic (DZ) come from two separate fusions of ova and sperms. Their genetic inheritance is like that between two siblings born at different times.

Thus similarities in characteristics shown to be present in monozygotic twins are contributed mainly by their common genetic inheritance, and any differences are more easily accounted for by the contribution of the environment. The similarities and differences of the DZ twins are accounted for by the influences of genes and environment and do not allow the clear differentiation between nature and nurture to be made which MZ twins offer.

This experiment placed by nature at the disposal of scientists has been used to study the specific contribution of genes to depressive illness. In a review of the subject[5] which appeared in 1968 seven studies from different countries comprising 97 MZ and 119 DZ pairs of twins showed that the concordance or similarity rate for the presence of an affective illness in the other twin of an MZ pair was 68 per cent compared with 32 per cent for the DZ pair. The evidence in support of a genetic contribution is strong but not foolproof. There is still the possibility that factors in the family upbringing might have contributed to the high similarity rate of the MZ pair. When a further study was made of MZ twins reared apart, the high concordance rate was still observed.

It will be noticed, however, that even in the MZ pairs the similarity rate is short of 100 per cent. This might be partially accounted for by the fact that the identical twin of the affected brother or sister may still show evidence of the illness some years after the time of the completion of the study since it is known that the disease may manifest itself after an interval of many years. Even when allowance is made for this, the similarity rate does not reach complete identity and the conclusion at this stage must be that although genetic influences do undoubtedly exist, there is no certain and absolute genetic determination.

Given that there is a genetic element, what is its mode of inheritance? The answer has been summed up thus by a leading authority.

It is easier to show how the predisposition is not transmitted than how it is. First of all, it is not to any significant extent transmitted as a recessive character. With recessive inheritance there are more affected siblings than either parents or children and this is not the case with affective disorders, where the figures for all classes of first degree relatives are very similar. With rare recessive genes an excess of cousin marriages is found among the parents, and this has not been found with affective disorders. On the other hand, transmission as a fully penetrant dominant Mendelian character can also be ruled out, as the risks in first degree relatives are well below the expected 50 per cent. Sex-linked inheritance can also be excluded with reasonable confidence, in spite of several claims to the contrary.[6]

Thus pure, recessive, dominant modes of inheritance are not the answer. What is currently considered likely is a polygenic model. That is to say, many genes combine in action to produce a vulnerable predisposition.

Some of the genetic influence may operate via the type of body build. Information is rather scarce but some link has been shown between bodily shape, personality, and mood. The work of Kretschmer[7] and Sheldon[8] has attempted, with some success, to relate bodily configuration and temperament. Kretschmer (in 1936) classified temperament according to body builds which consisted of the pyknic, leptosomic, athletic and dysplastic variety. The pyknic person is short and has a rotund figure with a broad face similar to the John Bull configuration. This body build has been associated with an outgoing, extrovert personality and a tendency to cyclothymic changes of mood from depression to elation, linked with the manic-depressive psychosis. The leptosomic physique is the opposite: a tall, thin person with a flat, narrow chest. Introverts are more often of this type and the suggestion is that they are more often susceptible to the other major psychosis of schizophrenia. Sheldon refined these measurements into three basic physical types: endomorph (chiefly gut and viscera), mesomorph (chiefly muscle and bone) and ectomorph (chiefly linearity). In this grouping the endomorphic form is associated with manic-depressive psychosis, and the ectomorphic physique with schizophrenia. It should be noted that these conclusions are based on averaging a large number of measurements and that, although statistically they hold some truth, the evidence is too limited to go beyond generalizations at this stage.

BIOCHEMISTRY

The conclusion that genetic influences contribute to depressive illnesses does not indicate how they operate. For this a clearer picture is needed of how mood changes occur at the biological level. To link the subjective inner world of mood and feelings with the biochemistry of the nervous and endocrine systems may seem an attempt to bridge an impossible gap, but in fact some of the most promising information about the nature of mood has been emerging from biologically based research on man and animals. This research is beginning to unravel some of the complicated threads of the physical basis of depressive illness.

The story is relatively recent and begins in the early fifties when it was noticed that a drug called reserpine, which was given to patients for high blood pressure, was causing in some 10-12 per cent of patients severe depressive symptoms and some suicides were reported. This chance finding brought the topic within the grasp of pharmacologists and biochemists who were able to investigate the connection further.

In 1957 Carlsson and his co-workers[9] showed that reserpine depleted all body cells of certain monoamines. Monoamines, which are organic compounds containing nitrogen, are separated into catecholamines known as noradrenaline (NA) and dopamine (DA), and indoleamines known as 5 hydroxytryptamine (5H.T.) called serotonin. Animal studies showed that reserpine which caused depletion of 5H.T. and NA was accompanied by decreased concentration and also sedation. Increased monoamines, on the other hand, produced excitation. These marked behaviour changes in animals associated with the monoamines, became the subject of further extensive research into the human mood changes associated with depression and elation.

Another chance finding based on clinical observation took place in 1951. A new drug called iproniazid was being used to combat tuberculosis. Marked improvement was noticed which was also found in treated patients with advanced cancer. In both instances there were mood changes but in the opposite direction to reserpine: the drug raised the mood, combated depression and even stimulated euphoric changes. This resulted in the birth in 1956 of the first antidepressant drug, Iproniazid. Furthermore, it was known that Iproniazid inhibited an enzyme called monoamine oxidase which is related to the breakdown of the monoamines. As a result of inhibiting the breakdown of the monoamines their quantity increased and this brought about a reversal of the depressive mood. Iproniazid was the first of the other compounds which formed a class of antidepressants which are called the monamine oxidase inhibitors or the MAOI (See Chapter XIV).

Thus it is only some twenty years ago that the biochemical breakthrough in understanding depression began in earnest. The precise location of the monoamines is still being investigated, but the brain appears to be the principal site. The three monoamines are not uniformly distributed throughout the brain. NA is present in greater concentration in the hypothalamus and brain stem; DA in the corpus striatum and 5H.T. in the same areas as NA and in parts of the limbic system.

The hypothesis that all this research led to was formulated as follows:

> Some, if not all, depressions are associated with an absolute or relative deficiency of catecholamines, particularly noradrenaline, at functionally important adrenergenic receptors in the brain. Elation conversely may be associated with an excess of such amines.[10]

Other biochemical research has pointed to a link between depressive illness and the adrenal gland. Research over a long period has indicated a link between brain centres of the hypothalamus and the pituitary and peripheral organs, like the thyroid, ovaries and adrenal glands. The importance of the adrenal gland lies in the fact that some of its secretions, like adrenaline, are similar compounds to the catecholamines found in the brain, and other substances emanating from its cortex play an important part in stress. The adrenal gland, which is situated in the abdomen, is part of a complex internal system of adaption to stress linked to the pituitary and hypothalamus situated in the brain. These organs form what has come to be described as the hypothalamic-pituitary-adrenal axis – a vital controlling system through which the regulation of the instinctual, emotional and affective behaviour occurs. The release of adrenal cortex hormones are ultimately related to general health and to anxiety reactions. Repeated studies suggest that some depressive patients:

(1) have defective regulation of their hypothailamic-pituitary-adrenal control mechanisms;
(2) excrete high amounts of active hydrocortisone from the adrenal gland.

Clearly we need to know a great deal more about all this but, since the link between hypothalamus, pituitary and adrenal cortex plays an important part in adaptation in man – particularly under stress – any basic disturbance which appears to be present in relation to depression is of significance.

These biological studies of depression are still at an early stage and yet the future management of depressive illnesses depends on the successful accumulation of reliable information. The biological research can be considered as one of the major advances in the field of psychiatry and medicine, even though its contribution can only be a part of the whole picture.

Another important aspect of depression is the dynamic element. By this is meant the person's emotional experiences accumulated in the course of their development with particular reference to the links they have formed with such key people as their parents, brothers, sisters, relatives and friends. This is part of the contribution of 'nurture' to the personality, playing a major share in human joy and misery, the latter being intimately linked with depression. The principal features of these interpersonal experiences which are linked with depression will be considered next.

Notes

1. Baillarger, J., (1854), 'Note sur un quere de folie dont les accès sont caracterisés par deux periodes régulieres, l'une de depression et l'autre d'excitation,' *Gazette Hebdomadaire de Sciences Medicales de Bordeaux*, (Paris), 1,263 and 279

2. Falret, J. P., (1854), 'Sur la folie circulaire,' *Bull. Acad. Med.*, Paris, 19,382-400

3. Price, J. S., (1968), 'The Genetics of Depressive Behaviour' in *Recent Developments in Affective Disorders*, Royal Medico-Psychological Association

4. Wilson, D. C., (1951), *Diseases of the Nervous System*, 12,363

5. Price, J. S., (1968), *op. cit.*

6. Price, J. S., (1968), *Hospital Medicine 2*, 1172

7. Kretschmer, E., (1936), *Physique and Character*, Second Ed. revised, Miller, London

8. Sheldon, W. H., Tucker, W. B., (1942), *The Varieties of Temperament*, London and New York

9. Carlsson, A., (1959), *Pharmacological Review*, 11, 490-93

10. Schildkraut, J. J., Kety, S. S., (1967), *Biogenic Amines and Emotion Science*, 156, 2

V The Significance and Meaning of Mood
2: *Dynamic Considerations*

Advances in genetic, physical and biochemical knowledge provide us with an awareness of the biological infrastructure associated with changes in mood. Such knowledge, however, does not and cannot by itself tell us what aspects of human experience initiate and maintain such physical changes unless it is assumed that these always occur spontaneously, subject to their own internal mechanisms, and remain unrelated to the course of our daily lives. But no one makes such a claim. Nor, were it made, could it be sustained, for ordinary experience plainly contradicts it. But what specific aspects of living provoke a depressive response?

Dynamic psychology is concerned with the development and exchange of feelings, emotions and instincts. The first and crucial observation was the linking of depression with the sense of loss; more specifically, depression was seen as a process similar to mourning and grief. Freud was aware both of the difficulties in definition and the likely physical basis of depression (frequently called melancholia in those days). In 1917 he wrote:

> Melancholia, whose definition fluctuates even in descriptive psychiatry, takes on various forms, the grouping together of which into a single unity does not seem to be established with certainty; and some of these forms suggest somatic rather than psychogenic affections . . . The correlation of melancholia and mourning seems justified by the general picture of the two conditions. Moreover, the exciting causes due to environmental influences are, so far as we can discern them at all, the same for both conditions. Mourning is regularly the reaction to the loss

of a loved person, or to the loss of some abstraction
which has taken the place of one, such as one's country,
liberty, an ideal and so on. In some people the same
influences produce melancholia instead of mourning . . .[1]

Conscious of the (still unresolved) problems of definition
and aware that there probably were contributory factors, he
nevertheless went on to formulate a psychological explanation to account for the general impoverishment and low
degree of self-esteem so typical of depression.

In mourning, the grief is related to the pain experienced
through the loss of a loved person or a precious object. In
the period of grief, the mourner withdraws into himself, lives
inwardly, nursing hurt feelings, not particularly interested
in new contacts, his attention focused on his loss. Gradually
the intensity of pain lessens and, in terms of Freudian
theory, libido or psychic energy is gradually withdrawn
from the lost object. In psychoanalytical language the word
'object' usually refers to a person and so can be confused
with the inanimate object usually intended. Gradually reality
takes over, life demands readjustment, a return to ordinary
activities, and the establishment of new relationships. The
disengagement with the lost object is slow but is gradually
completed.

In depression there are the same features of painful dejection, reduction of activity and involvement, absence of interest
in others or in other things. But, in addition, there is something else which is not found in mourning, namely a marked
loss of self-respect, a diminution of self-regard. Freud goes
on to point out that, in contrast to grief, the depressed
person behaves as if what is lost is part of himself or, in
technical language, the object-loss becomes an ego-loss.
Furthermore, while in mourning what is lost is conscious, in
depression it may be conscious but is often unconscious. This
process has been described as follows:

If a person . . . feels, without being aware of such
feelings, that he would like to *be* what attracts him in the
object, or that he would like to *have* something from the
object for himself, not only the loss of such an object,

but any interferences with this object-relationship, a disappointment, a mere hurt, a feeling of neglect, of being out of favour, whether real or imaginary, will bring about a situation of catastrophic deprivation, particularly in early childhood. The first and foremost consequence of such experiences will be a lowering of self-regard and self-esteem, a feeling of self-depreciation.[2]

The word catastrophic applies to all situations in human relationships where the wholeness of our self depends on the positive availability of another person. In childhood it is often the parents who provide the first intimate relationship and in doing so establish the pattern for future relationships with relatives, spouse, friends and acquaintances. The support of those close to us is the basis of our continuous affirmation of our individuality and its absence a continuous source of threatened loss and depression. Clearly the greater the sense of personal wholeness and firm identity the less is the likelihood that withdrawal of approval will stimulate a depressive reaction but this is the achievement of a lifetime's work and, while clearly people will vary in their vulnerability, no man – as Donne said – is an island.

Freud developed the notion of libido and formulated the view that the development of the human personality ultimately depended on two basic instinctual forces, Eros and Thanatos, the first being the libido or life instinct and the second aggression or the death instinct. This purely theoretical model has been enormously influential in psychology, but the concept of psychic energy is not capable of exact scientific measurement and remains incapable of proof or disproof in its founder's terms. However other aspects of Freudian theory such as the emphasis placed on the significance of the early years, the relationship between child and parents, emotional trauma, intrapsychic and interpersonal conflict, and the unconscious have stood the test of time and are now being reformulated within modern concepts.

One of these concepts has been emphasized by Dr John Bowlby[3] who has insisted that the most significant event in early life is the bond formed between child and mother.

Bowlby is himself a psychoanalyst but, discarding the libido theory, he has instead proposed a specific biological model whose psychological implications are enormous. For him the child forms by the sixth month of life a specific attachment to its mother brought about by an exchange of contact mediated through vision, sound and touch. Although feeding is clearly important in this process, it is the interaction based on visual recognition, the familiarity of uniquely distinguishable sounds, and sheer physical accessibility that forges a bond, an attachment, the foundation of security. The loss of such a bond leads to anxiety, sorrow, and anger.

The way to avoid this distressing reaction is to ensure that there is no prolonged absence or, as it has come to be called, maternal deprivation during the early years. The child can take increasing periods of separation without distress from about the age of three onwards, but prolonged disruption of the attachment without adequate substitute surrogate persons produces a sequence of distress that has been described as protest, despair and detachment. Here is how Bowlby describes it:

The initial phase, that of protest, may begin immediately or may be delayed; it lasts from a few hours to a week or more. During it the young child appears acutely distressed at having lost his mother and seeks to recapture her by the full exercise of his limited resources. He will often cry loudly, shake his cot, throw himself about, and look eagerly towards any sight or sound which might prove to be his missing mother. All his behaviour suggests strong expectations that she will return. Meanwhile he is apt to reject all alternative figures who offer to do things for him though some children will cling desperately to a nurse.

During the phase of despair, which succeeds protest, the child's preoccupation with his missing mother is still evident, though his behaviour suggests increasing hopelessness. The active physical movements diminish or come to an end, and he may cry monotonously or intermittently. He is withdrawn and inactive, makes no demands on people in the environment, and appears to be in a state of deep mourning. This is a quiet stage, and sometimes, clearly erroneously, is presumed to indicate a diminution of distress.

Because the child shows more interest in his surroundings, the phase of detachment which sooner or later succeeds protest and despair is often welcomed as a sign of recovery. The child no longer rejects the nurses; he accepts their care and the food and toys they bring, and may even smile and be sociable. To some this change seems satisfactory. When his mother visits, however, it can be seen that all is not well, for there is a striking absence of the behaviour characteristic of the strong attachment normal at this age. So far from greeting his mother he may seem hardly to know her; so far from clinging to her he may remain remote and apathetic; instead of tears there is a listless turning away. He seems to have lost all interest in her.

Should his stay in hospital or residential nursery be prolonged and should he, as is usual, have the experience of becoming transiently attached to a series of nurses each of whom leaves and so repeats for him the experience of the original loss of his mother, he will in time act as if neither mothering nor contact with humans had much significance for him. After a series of upsets at losing several mother-figures to whom in turn he has given some trust and affection, he will gradually commit himself less and less to succeeding figures and in time will stop altogether attaching himself to anyone. He will become increasingly self-centred and, instead of directing his desires and feelings towards people, will become preoccupied with material things such as sweets, toys and food. A child living in an institution or hospital who has reached this state will no longer be upset when nurses change or leave. He will cease to show feelings when his parents come and go on visiting day; and it may cause them pain when they realize that although he has an avid interest in the presents they bring, he has little interest in them as special people. He will appear cheerful and adapted to his unusual situation and apparently easy and unafraid of anyone. But this sociability is superficial; he appears no longer to care for anyone.[4]

This basic account of attachment and detachment, with the intervening depression, refers to the life of a child in a hospital or other institution and is clearly rare. But from time to time millions of viewers are subjected through television to the agonizing scene of children being forcibly separated from a foster mother, having been claimed by their own mother. No one will doubt the suffering caused by the disruption of such a close relationship, whether in childhood or later in life. The distress it causes in childhood is particularly strong because of the child's inability to cope with the loss. But the process Bowlby describes is a crucial one at all times and there can be no doubt that here we have a psychological mechanism linked with grief, sorrow and distress that has the widest repercussions in all human relationships at whatever age. It will be examined repeatedly throughout this book.

A great deal of argument surrounds the concept of maternal deprivation and recently the subject has been excellently reviewed by Professor M. Rutter.[5] As far as the relationship between depression and separation is concerned there is evidence that, beyond the immediate distress, the disruption in continuity and familiarity is associated with depression. This has been found in children when there is a loss of one parent and the child has been placed in a foster home, but not in those losing a parent but remaining with the other parent, so that bond disruption may not be the principal cause of subsequent depression.[6]

Depression in adult life has been linked with the disruption of bonds in childhood and adolescence even though the evidence is not clear-cut.[7][8][9] If a wider view of disruption of personal bonds is taken, evidence has been presented that depression and suicide are associated with recent bereavement,[10] marital breakdown[11][12] and moving to a new neighbourhood.

The formation, disruption, loss and reconstruction of personal bonds form one of the mainsprings of human activity and there is abundant subjective and increasingly objective scientific evidence that these processes are intimately linked with sorrow, grief and the expenditure of much suffering whose reality lends itself far more to objective measurement than Freud's libido theory. Thus it can be confidently expected that our understanding of the depressive process will continue to increase as further research in this area is carried out.

Returning to the libido theory, however, provides us with a possible explanation of another aspect of depressive symptomatology. In the book *Anxiety and Neurosis* Dr Rycroft writes:

> The melancholic behaves not only as though he had lost someone but also as though he were himself responsible for this loss and he therefore suffers not only grief but also guilt and remorse.[18]

One aspect of the libido theory attempts to explain the loss of self-esteem, the other the presence of guilt and remorse by introducing the concept of conflict, ambivalence and the expression of aggression. The person we are attached to, the person we love, is also the person who deprives us of the good experiences we wish to have with them. They deny, deprive, punish us as parents, relations, friends and spouses and we retaliate by expressing our aggression towards them. This aggression may be real, but even if it exists only in our imagination the fantasy may extend to the belief that we have inflicted irreparable damage which causes us to feel guilty and depressed. Similarly the depression may be associated with equivalent hostility which is now no longer directed towards an object but is turned inwardly towards ourselves. Such self-hate may ultimately be responsible not only for depression and guilt but also for self-destruction in the form of suicide.

The early theorizing of Karl Abraham[14] on this topic was taken up later on by another equally noted psychoanalyst, Melanie Klein. Pursuing the theory of the death instinct, she traced the theoretical beginnings of its expression in the first six months of life and described two psychological situations technically called 'positions'.

The beginning of life is an utterly threatening experience full of anxiety and the child is meant to cope with this anxiety by a process known technically as splitting. In the first three months it has no concept of its mother as a whole person; its attention is focused on parts of the body and, since feeding is so important, particularly on the breast. The breast is the source of life, it is good or bad, it feeds, it does not feed. Life, which is either good or bad, is split neatly into these two categories. There are no gradations. The fear at this stage is supposed to be that the ego of the child will be overwhelmed by bad feelings linked with the breast which represents the whole of the mother. This anxiety is called persecutory anxiety, hence the name given to the position of the child in the first three months as paranoid. The ego defends itself against such anxiety by splitting its experiences. It preserves its good ones and projects or pushes out its bad ones. Persecutory anxiety not only comes from the inside world of the child when in fantasy it feels as if it has chewed up the breast (which represents mother) to pieces, but also from the outside world when mother or someone in her place fails to give the baby the safety and care it needs.

This persecutory anxiety can thus be felt emanating from the mother herself, from the bad feelings inside the baby or from the bad feelings pushed out or projected in the mother which are then experienced as rebounding back from her. At this early stage there is no way of dealing with all this nastiness other than by throwing it out, projecting it, and freezing the ego from such bad feelings. By this defensive manoeuvring the goodness of mother and self can be retained through splitting which allows the separation of feelings into completely different departments. Mother is totally good or bad, the baby is totally good or bad. There are no alternatives.

In the following three months the child's attitude changes. According to Klein, the child now begins to recognize the whole of its mother, and of course its father as well. This relationship to the whole person has been described as the 'Depressive position'. In it the child recognizes its ambivalence. It hates and loves the same person. But in doing this

D

the child is no longer afraid that its own ego will be destroyed by threatening objects of a persecuting nature impinging from outside as in the paranoid-schizoid position, but rather that its own aggression will destroy the fantasy of a good mother now present in its own ego. It now begins to feel guilty that its aggression has been able to destroy and lose mother, a guilt feeling of course which can be reinforced by mother's attitude later on. This destruction remains oral in character meaning that mother has been taken in and chewed up in pieces inside the child.

Alongside the feeling of loss and misery over this destruction in fantasy, there is now an equal feeling of reparation, once again in fantasy. Love can repair the damage and restore the wholeness of the pieces.

Many have criticized Klein for using these somewhat confusing terms. Everybody realizes that such a theory cannot ever be tested, proved or disproved and certainly we have no idea whether all this takes place in the first six months of life. All that can definitely be seen is that by six months there is recognition and firm attachment to the mother figure. Nevertheless there is clinical evidence that all the mechanisms that Klein describes are in fact used by older people and certainly the cycle of aggression, fear of damage, real or imagined, guilt, reparation sequences and the accompanying relief of guilt and depression are common human experiences which, even if they do not occur in the first six months of life, certainly are acquired early in childhood. It is certainly a cycle which traditional morality seems to have used as a model for repairing the human capacity to hurt and damage others.

The psychological mechanisms described provide between them wide ranging possibilities of understanding human interaction associated with depression as well as providing a readily available framework for understanding some of the consequences of conflict in interpersonal activity.

Notes

1. Freud, S., (1917), *Mourning and Melancholia* in the Standard Edition, Vol. xiv, Translated by James Strachey, Hogarth Press, London
2. Hoffer, W., (1964), *Psychology and Psychotherapy in Depression*, Ed. by E. Beresford Davies, Cambridge University Press
3. Bowlby, John, (1969), *Attachment and Loss,* Vol. I, The International Psychoanalytical Library, No. 79, Hogarth Press, London
4. *Ibid.,* pp. 27-8
5. Rutter, M., (1972), *Maternal Deprivation,* Penguin Books, Harmondsworth
6. Caplan, M. A., Douglas, V. I., (1969), 'Incidence of parental loss in children with depressed mood', *Journal of Child Psychology and Psychiatry,* 10:225
7. Rutter, M., (1971), 'Parent Child Separation: Psychological effects on the children', *Journal of Child Psychology and Psychiatry,* 12:233
8. Hill, O., (1972), 'Childhood Bereavement and Adult Psychiatric Disturbances,' *Journal of Psychological Research*
9. Alkon, D. L., (1971), 'Parental Deprivation', *Acta Psychiatrica Scandinavica* supplement 223
10. Young, M., Benjamin, B., Wallis, C., (1963), 'The Mortality of Widowers', *Lancet,* II, 454
11. Paykel, E. S., et al., (1971), 'Scaling of Life Events', *Archives of General Psychiatry,* 25,340
12. Schless, A. P., *et al.,* (1974), 'How Depressives view the significance of Life Events', *British Journal of Psychiatry,* 125, 406
13. Rycroft, C., (1970), *Anxiety and Neurosis,* Pelican, p. 47
14. Abraham, K., (1911), 'Notes on the psychoanalytical investigation and treatment of manic-depressive insanity and allied disorders', *Selected papers,* London, Hogarth Press & Institute of Psychoanalysis 1942: 137

VI Epidemiology of Depression

Following the descriptions of possible causes of depression, it is interesting to inquire how many people – and of what sex and age – suffer from this condition. For those who are subject to mood changes and suffer from them this question is of little interest. It is enough for them that *they* suffer from it and it is little comfort to know that others share their misery. However this knowledge is helpful to many people in their continuous battle for reassurance that their condition does not reflect some individual peculiarity which singles them out from others. Besides this personal element, the incidence of depression is of vital importance in assessing the provisions needed for an adequate medical service on an outpatient and inpatient basis. The science of studying these characteristics is known as epidemiology. Understandably the statistics concerning depression are not likely to be precise or clearcut.

We have already noted the problems of definition, to which have to be added the widely prevailing differences in defining the criteria of a 'case'. Who does one place in the category of depression? The person with fleeting mood changes, who does not consult a doctor, those who consult him on an isolated occasion, those who consult him frequently? Should a distinction be made between new referrals and cases already known to exist in the community? Over what sort of period are new referrals to be calculated?

Some of the answers are self-evident. We cannot know anything about depression if the victim does not report his state to someone who has some understanding of it. This is usually the family doctor, the hospital service or a special research team. Already this narrows down the possibility of our having an accurate knowledge of the numbers who are prone to this condition because some sufferers will not report to anybody, thus preventing our having an accurate number for those who are subject to mood swings. Inevitably the available figures reflect those who are sufficiently worried about their symptoms to seek help. Since it is generally supposed that some doctors have a reputation for being more sympathetic to nervous conditions, it is important to make assessments over a wide cross section of doctors representing different outlooks. This has been done and it can be said with some certainty that the data available reflect reasonably accurately the situation as it affects those whose depression is severe enough to seek at least one consultation with a doctor.

But even at the medical level a distinction must be made between those seen by general practitioners and those referred to hospital physicians, particularly psychiatrists. Those seen in hospital undoubtedly represent the most severely disabled, particularly if inpatients are considered. With these reservations in mind we can now look at the available information.

HOSPITALIZATION

Admission figures for depressive psychoses in mental hospitals and psychiatric units of general hospitals covering the years 1964 to 1969 show that the numbers admitted annually per 100,000 of the population range between 79-88 for men and 152-167 for women.[1] Two aspects are worthy of note: first that depression heads the list of mental illnesses which necessitated admission, followed closely by schizophrenia, both of which are a three to four times more frequent reason for admission than most other diagnostic categories. When it is remembered that mental illness accounted for 31 per cent of the average number of beds occupied daily in the hospital service (for the year 1970), then clearly depression plays a very big part in psychiatric illness requiring hospital admission.

Secondly these figures show, in a striking way, what most surveys confirm, that depressive illness is far more common in women than in men; in fact the admission rate for women is about double.

A more detailed analysis[2] was made of first-ever inpatient admissions to the National Health Service hospital psychiatric service for the two years 1965 and 1966. In this study emphasis is given to age and type of affective disorder with both sexes combined.

TABLE II

Age	Mania	Depression
16	104	1864
20	162	3847
25	143	4254
30	197	4421
35	189	5121
40	228	5993
45	215	5750
50	269	6146
55	233	6113
60	257	5624
65	192	4477
70	155	2696
75 and over	212	2288
Totals	2,556	58,594

When Table II is considered two main features stand out. Firstly, manic illness is a much rarer event than depression: secondly, both mania and depression are illnesses which increase with age until the sixth decade. The starting point at the age of sixteen is accounted for by the fact that the numbers were compiled from adult admissions, but for a long time there was a widespread view that children were not likely to be victims of depression. This view is now altering and the subject will be considered in Chapter VII.

REFERRAL TO GENERAL PRACTITIONER

Not every one suffering from a mood disturbance who is seen in a hospital outpatient clinic is admitted as an inpatient; more importantly, those referred to a hospital are in turn a small fraction of those who consult their family doctor. Thus consultation rates of general practitioners are likely to give a truer picture of the extent of affective disorders. A number of studies exist which attempt to answer this question.[3 4 5 6 7]

These studies were carried out amongst general practices in London, Birmingham, Leicestershire, North Scotland and Surrey. It has been estimated that the average figure from these inquiries produces rates which are ten times greater than the rate for psychiatric hospital admission in 1960 in England and Wales.[8] Even if we allow for the limitations of such studies and comparisons there is still a notable ten-fold increase in prevalence. This leaves us with the most difficult question of all to tackle, namely the incidence of depression which is sufficiently severe to make a recognizable impact on the individual but is not severe enough for him to visit a doctor. Such a study would be most difficult to conduct since this would require giving a strict definition of a depressive period. Would a matter of hours, days or weeks qualify? What sort of intensity would be required to qualify? Such obstacles can be overcome up to a point, at which stage it can be expected that a further increase in incidence will be found.

Despite the inherent difficulties in such a study, one was nevertheless carried out in Sweden in 1947 when a survey was made of the past and present mental health of the entire population of two adjacent parishes in Southern Sweden. In 1957 the same population was studied again and individuals who had left were traced. Under such close scrutiny and with the inclusion of milder cases, a higher incidence could be expected and was indeed found. When estimating the lifetime risk of depression[9] they found that for men the risk was 8.5 per cent and for women 17.7 per cent. A risk of the order of one in ten in the population found by these studies is also confirmed in one British study.[10]

If the risk of having an affective illness is generally of the order of one in ten in the population, bearing in mind the higher rate for women, by what age can one hope to have escaped the illness? It has been noted that the figures for affective illnesses steadily rise with age and that furthermore, unlike other mental disorders such as schizophrenia and neurosis, they do not tend to decline in the second half of life. In fact current research indicates that between 70 and 90 per cent of the risk is passed only at the age of sixty-five.[11][12]

All these calculations have to negotiate the problems of the uncertainty of classification and the appropriate criteria for measurement so that as far as possible observations from different sources are all measuring the same thing. In a subject which attracts so much controversy in classification, it is remarkable that the data presented in this chapter were achieved at all. They represent the determined efforts made in Europe, particularly in the Scandinavian countries and in Britain. It is more difficult to assess data from the USA because in addition to the classification problems, there has been a tendency for American psychiatrists to diagnose schizophrenia in cases where a European psychiatrist would choose a depressive diagnosis and so comparison between the two countries has to make allowances for such an in-built bias.

Despite the variety and complexity of classification, the evidence does suggest strongly that affective disorder in the form of depression is a prominent contribution to ill health and the breakthrough in treatment that has been achieved in the last twenty years represents one of the most important revolutions in medicine which, if not exactly parallel, can certainly be compared to the advent of the antibiotic era which has made such a difference in the treatment of infection.

Before discussing treatment, however, we should give consideration to some of the reasons responsible for the steady increase in incidence of depression with each successive decade until retirement. These years cover adolescence, sexual maturity, reproduction and marriage, the middle years and retirement age with its rising incidence of loss of the spouse. In all these periods certain crucial happenings stand out as possible sources of stress which, interacting with a vulnerable predisposition, result in a depressive illness. Common sense dictates that such stresses could produce a depressive outcome and recent work has tended to prove this.

In the next few chapters these periods will be considered in turn beginning with childhood. This period was traditionally considered to be free of depressive episodes, a view which has been disproved by recent studies.

Notes

1. H.M.S.O., (1972), *Social Trends*, No. 3, Table 63, 'Hospitals selected psychiatric illness', London
2. Spicer, C. C., Hare, E. H., Slater, E., (1973), 'Neurotic and Psychotic Forms of Depressive Illness', *British Journal of Psychiatry*, 123, 535
3. Shepherd, M., Cooper, B., Brown, A. C., Kniton, G. W., (1966), *Psychiatric Illness in General Practice*, Oxford University Press
4. Watts, C. A. H., (1966), *Depressive Disorders in the Community*, Bristol
5. Crombie, D. L., (1957), *General Practitioner Research Newsletter*, No. 16, 218
6. Primrose, E. J. R., (1962), *Psychological Illness; A community study*, London
7. Porter, A. M. W., (1970), 'Depressive Illness in a General Practice', *Brit. Med. Journal*, 773
8. Rawnsley, K., (1968), 'Epidemiology of Affective Disorder in recent developments in Affected Disorders.' *Royal Medico-psychological Association*
9. Essen-Moller, Hagnell, O., (1961), 'The frequency and risk of depression within a rural population group in Scania', *Acta Psychiatrica Scandinavica*, Supplement 162, 37
10. Watts, C. A. H., *op. cit.*
11. Norris, V., (1959), Mental Illness in London, Maudsley Monographs. No. 6, London
12. Fremming, G. H., (1951), 'The expectation of mental infirmity in a sample of the Danish population', *Occasional Paper of the Eugenics Society*, London, No. 7

VII   Childhood and Adolescence

If childhood is described as the period covering the pre-school and school years then the task of definition is reasonably simple. By comparison adolescence, which is associated with puberty but not initiated by it, is a blurred period, without precise onset or conclusion. Thus, somewhat arbitrarily, this chapter will deal with depression covering the period between birth until the presumed conclusion of adolescence with the beginning of marriage which is on average twenty-four for men and twenty-two for women.

CHILDHOOD

In Chapter V a description was given of the similarity noted by Freud between depression and mourning and by some further extrapolation mourning was advanced to its earliest phase when the young baby 'grieves' for the loss of mother when she absents herself. This is a loss that can be coped with satisfactorily if it is brief but becomes a major challenge related to a depressive reaction if – in the first few years of life – it is prolonged.

Some of the earliest systematic observations on young children facing maternal separation were carried out during and after the Second World War. Most of these were made on very young infants in institutions such as hospitals, orphanages or prisons. In a wide-ranging review of depression in childhood, Henry Balkwin, Professor of Clinical Paediatrics in the New York University School of Medicine, makes the remarkable statement that in the first decade or two of this century the death rate in institutions for the care of infants was virtually one hundred per cent. Here are his own words:

At one of these institutions, the admission card of each

little patient carried the designation 'desperately ill' although he may have been a chubby rosy baby. The phenomenon of the emotionally deprived baby — referred to as hospitalismus — was widespread. It was seen in all parts of the United States, in Europe and Latin America as well. Although the babies were offered diets adequate for proper weight gain in the home, they withered away in the institution and died. Usually they accepted the food offered; nevertheless they failed to gain weight and often lost it. Apathy, listlessness, pallor, a loss of sucking habits, immobility, frequent stools and fitful sleep were other features . . .

The prompt change that took place when these babies were transferred to the care of a warm and attentive mother or mother substitute was striking. One such baby who, at four months, weighed only as much as he had at birth; who looked like a tiny, wizened old man; and who looked as though he might lie and stop breathing at any time, was, nevertheless, sent home. When I visited him in his home 24 hours after discharge from the hospital I could hear him cooing in an adjoining room. From the day he reached home he started to gain weight — on the same formula prescribed in the hospital — and continued to progress so that by the end of the first year his weight was in the normal range and his development was normal in every other respect.[1]

This *marasmus* of the first few months is accounted for by the loss of sensory stimulation, the lack of contact and playing with mother or nurse. Soon, however, another psychological happening occurs, also described in Chapter V, namely the bonding process, the formation of a powerful attachment to mother. Once this bond has been formed there is a grieving sequence which is intensely powerful and which has been shown to go through a sequence of protest, despair and detachment. Although there are theoretical differences in the underlying assumptions, described by various authors, these depressive reactions were first noted in the first year of life by Spitz and Wolf who studied one hundred infants of unmarried mothers in a prison in the United

States, who were separated from their mothers in the third
and fourth quarter of the first year of life. The reactions
of these babies were observed and were described as
anaclitic depressions,[2] showing features of misery, lack of
expression and withdrawal. In this country observations containing similar clinical descriptions were made during the
war by Anna Freud, the daughter of Sigmund Freud, and
Dorothy Burlingham which were published in the form of
two books.[3][4] Since then there has been continuing work
in this area emphasizing the importance of preserving the
links between children and parents or in the event of separation adequate parent surrogates. This care is particularly
important in the case of hospitalization of young children.
The concept of depression arising out of separation anxiety
is now an established phenomenon and much practical work
has been done in the hospital service to encourage parental
attendance, thus avoiding distress to children.

While adult depression can certainly be accounted for on
some occasions by a precisely similar loss of personal relationship, clearly there are other contributory factors of a
constitutional and environmental nature. The point of interest
here is to inquire whether depression can be seen in children,
contributed to by similar characteristics as in adults, i.e.
genetic disposition, but not accounted for by the process of
separation or loss of personal attachments.

Although occasionally the problem has been referred to by
earlier psychiatrists[5] the concept of depression in childhood
has only recently been described in Britain. Not surprisingly,
the criteria for diagnosis are still not agreed upon. In a
recent study a psychiatrist describes a typical depressive
picture in children which can begin as early as four to
six but is far more likely to be seen at about the age of
ten.

Irritability, weepiness and a tendency to recurrent ex-
plosions of temper or misery, which may have no adequate
other explanation, are the most characteristic features
. . . Nearly half of these children have difficulty in
getting off to sleep, or have a poor night, because of
restlessness, nightmares, sleepwalking, talking or scream-

ing. No less than a quarter wake in the middle of the night, or unusually early, in just the same way as do adult patients who are suffering from endogenous depressive illness. A sizeable number complain spontaneously of feeling depressed and express suicidal ideas, feelings and attempts.[6]

Not all the children do, in fact, express themselves clearly in this way and some present themselves with a persistent physical complaint such as loss of appetite, tummy pains, headaches or psychological features such as boredom, fatigue and lack of concentration.

The subject of suicidal attempts and suicide will be dealt with in Chapters XVII and XVIII for adults; the information available for children will be given here for the sake of completion of the topic. Suicidal attempts and suicide itself are undoubtedly rare, in fact as rare as depression in childhood but instances certainly do exist.

According to a historical account[7] suicide in children was first reported in Prussia late in the eighteenth century. There was an increase at the beginning of this century, decreasing until the mid-thirties with an upsurge since. Exact numbers are unknown. One of the largest and most comprehensive studies covered attempted suicides throughout the whole of Sweden during the five years between 1955 and 1959. The number involved was 1727 children, the youngest of whom was ten, the oldest twenty-one. In this material the author found that 80 per cent of those who attempted suicide were girls, but the boys actually ran a higher risk of committing suicide. Three to four suicidal attempts are made for each suicide by boys and between 25 and 30 by girls. A follow-up study of these same boys and girls, who were examined in 1960, was made up to fifteen years later and the seriousness of these attempts is reflected in the fact that a significantly higher proportion of those who had attempted suicide died than in a control group, in fact no less than 84 compared to 27.[8] In a recent study, all suicides of children under the age of fourteen which occurred in England and Wales between 1962 and 1968 were recorded. In all 31 children killed themselves giving an incidence of one child in 800,000 of the population.[9]

Not all suicidal threats in children need to be taken seriously. Children do make remarks such as 'I wish I was dead', 'What's the point of living?', 'You will be sorry when you lose your little girl', all of which are passing remarks in response to lack of attention, frustration or short-lived anger. When these same remarks, however, are repeated with a serious note injected in their proclamation then the situation is radically different and certainly when a gesture has been made it should never be lightly dismissed.[10]

In this country an annual estimate of between 1,204 and 1,600 suicidal attempts by children and adolescents has been suggested,[11] but clearly a great deal more research is needed to develop accurate statistics.

Statistics are not needed, however, to suggest that a combination of depressive predisposition and stress, particularly stress between parent and child, is the combination that builds the escalating tension that leads to the suicide attempt. The stress follows marked conflict exhibited between the parents themselves, inability on the part of parents or parent substitutes to show the minimum level of concern and involvement that the child requires or, if this care is available, the inability of the child to actually experience and receive it. Misunderstanding, conflict, indifference, cruelty or excessive punishment are usually the provocative ingredients as illustrated in the following case which comes from the United States and shows incidentally that suicide attempts can be made at a very early age.

I had the opportunity of observing a young boy who showed a severe degree of depression. The boy made repeated and serious suicidal attempts beginning at $3\frac{1}{2}$ years.

Henry was the oldest of three children. During pregnancy the mother had had a 'kidney condition' and was 'swollen'. He was born at term without difficulty. At five months he began to bang his head. This became worse with time, and he would strike his head against a hard object such as the floor or a stone whenever he was frustrated. At this time he was described as aggressive, negativistic, bossy, quarrelsome, talkative and over-active.

The first suicidal attempt was made at $3\frac{1}{2}$ years when he stepped out of a first-storey window. Shortly thereafter he was found hanging by his arms from the fire escape. About this time he fell down a flight of stairs and bruised his head. He was also injured in a revolving door. At four years, after a severe beating, he said he was going to jump out of the window. He repeated this threat whenever he got angry. The parents reply was to 'go ahead' . . .

At $5\frac{1}{2}$ years he jumped out of a seventh-storey window. He got up and tried to walk, but collapsed and was stuporous for five days. The small bones of one foot were broken. Recovery was complete. The mother was dull mentally and rather passive, the father was foreign born and was described as dictatorial towards the children. The boy was antagonistic towards his father and hated him. He was intensely and overtly jealous of his father's relationship with his mother. At the same time he seemed to feel guilty about his feelings and wanted to punish himself.

At $8\frac{1}{2}$ years Henry had not voiced any more suicidal threats or made any suicidal attempts but his behaviour was still troublesome. He was described as 'highly strung, uncooperative, very disobedient'. He had no interest in school and his schoolwork was poor. His resentment towards his father continued. At $13\frac{1}{2}$ he was still a 'terrific' problem. He was just getting by in his schoolwork, although he was a bright boy who should have done much better. He created disturbances in the classroom and seemed to enjoy flaunting authority. He was resentful towards his father, who now treated him gently and tenderly. The father was outwardly calm and easygoing. Henry fought with his mother continuously. He took a dim view of life, always assuming a pessimistic attitude and predicting the worst.[12]

This picture of defiance, boredom, loss of interest in life, difficulty in concentration and pessimism which can amount to an inner despair with pronounced feelings of depression with or without aggression and delinquent behaviour is a recurrent picture seen in a few young adolescents who may well attempt suicide.

The significance of attempted suicide in adults has been extensively described and will be considered in Chapter XVIII but it has been noted repeatedly that children have little capacity to deal with depressed feelings which need to be dispelled through action. Such action can be due to a variety of reasons. It can be a gesture of anger, a signal of distress, an attempt to seek and manipulate attention, gain love and affection or to punish parents or siblings. Very rarely the feeling is based on the desire to join a dead relative.

Statistics suggest that numerically the size of the problem of attempted suicide is tiny, although numbers can be dangerous concealers of urgent and deep personal suffering which a child has limited resources to cope with.

ADOLESCENCE

Adolescence is defined by the Shorter Oxford Dictionary as 'The process or condition of growing up; the period between childhood and maturity, extending from fourteen to twenty-five in males, from twelve to twenty-one in females.' There is no agreed definition of the exact chronology but the principal physical, social and psychological events which have to be negotiated by the adolescent are fairly clear.

(a) *Separation*. The central feature of adolescence is separation. One way of looking at human maturation is to see it as a process of gradual separation of children from their parents in the course of the first two decades of life. Maturation consists of physical, social, psychological and spiritual growth which the parents promote and sustain and the child shapes individually. By the time the second half of the second decade is reached, the overwhelming majority of boys and girls have reached a sufficient level of growth to sustain an independent existence. This usually involves physical separation, the capacity to leave home for short or long periods or permanently and to live in a separate abode. Social separation requires that adolescents form a balance between the attitude found in the family milieu and their own independent interpretation of political, educational, economic and social justice, goals and standards. Psychologically the separation means inevitably the presence of some feelings of isolation which may become acute and reach real loneliness, uncertainty and confusion, tinged with anxiety. Occasionally the adolescent also has guilt feelings for leaving behind lonely parents who are in need of his presence for their own survival.

The spiritual separation involves a seeking of values which will make sense of the new approach to the world. Several studies, particularly at the beginning of the twentieth century have shown that adolescence is a time of conversion,[13] perhaps of religious conversion but, as actual religious conversion is not common nowadays, more a time of intense reflection on the meaning and value of life.

(b) *Sexual Development.* Another essential component of adolescence is puberty. For the girl this implies the growth of her breasts and the advent of menstruation. For the boy, the growth of his penis and testicles, spontaneous nocturnal emissions and, for both of them, the challenge of masturbation. Sexual education has stressed the need for biological information to prepare for the advent of puberty. There are innumerable accounts to this very day of the surprise, shock, fear and perplexity of the first menstruation and fantasies surrounding it in the absence of adequate preparation. But vital as such accurate information is, the physical configuration and physiological events impinge most strongly at the level of feelings and emotions. The body changes but, at the heart of these changes, what is set in motion is a powerful psycho-biological attraction of the opposite sex.

Though he might not articulate it in precisely these terms, the adolescent lives in that indeterminate zone where he finds himself to be neither an adult nor a child. He asks in many ways – 'What am I?' It is at this time in a person's life that problems associated with confusion of identity may arise.

Erikson has contributed a great deal on the meaning

of the concept of identity and the various phases it goes
through in the development of the personality from cradle to
grave. In this passage he is distinguishing between personal
identity and ego identity:

> The conscious feeling of having a personal identity is based
> on two simultaneous observations: the perception of the
> selfsameness and continuity of one's existence in time and
> space and the perception of the fact that others recognize
> one's sameness and continuity. What I have called ego
> identity, however, covers more than the mere fact of exis-
> tence; it is, as it were, the ego quality of this existence.[14]

The adolescent has to negotiate a marked change in
physical appearance particularly as regards sex and his sense
of familiar continuity with his image can be severely strained.
He or she has to undergo a physical change that will determine the extent to which others will find them physically
attractive. The body is no longer just a physical entity: it
has now become a powerful force and of significance in
communicating with another person. Everyone is familiar with
the anxieties young people of both sexes have about their
personal appearance, preoccupations that moralists have
tended to condemn as vain. Deeper psychological insights
help us to see that moral labelling of this anxiety as pride,
egoism or self-centredness, intending to produce sufficient
shame and guilt to turn behaviour in the opposite direction, does not constructively assist development. In reality, the
condemned behaviour is frequently the outward expression
of inward confusion, fear and shame stemming from the
anxiety the person experiences regarding their own identity
and their standing in their own eyes and the estimation of
others.

Adolescent 'vanity' is frequently anxiety about personal
appearance and the uncertainty of being able to attract and
hold a person of the opposite sex; in extreme cases the
psychiatrist must cope with young people who are convinced
that their appearance is appalling and beyond redemption.
Where they have marked acne, obesity or some genuine dis-
figuration, they may in fact need attention. But frequently

adolescents complain of physical features such as grotesquely shaped teeth, nose, ears or breasts which are revealed by examination to be absolutely normal or merely minimal deviations from normality. The person is using a part of their body to express their intense anxiety about the doubts they have regarding their own attraction and acceptability to others.

A most attractive eighteen-year-old girl attended an outpatient clinic complaining of gross abnormality in the appearance of her nose. On arriving home from work she would change into a dressing-gown and not leave her bedroom except for meals. Such an anxiety about physical appearance is often accompanied by marked feelings of depression which are not easily relieved since the depression reflects the total lack of faith in one's ability to appeal to others, particularly those of the opposite sex. A sense of urgency and desperation pushes some of these youngsters to demand plastic surgery which of course, without careful consideration of the underlying psychological factors, may be of little use. Indeed, surgery may precipitate a crisis as the excuse for the depression is then taken away and the person has to face the fact that it was not their appearance that was and still is holding them back, but their own lack of self-confidence. Occasionally, however, plastic surgery may relieve the anxiety sufficiently to overcome diffidence about mixing with others and the subsequent establishment of social contact lifts the depression almost magically.

Another less common but nonetheless important sexual contribution to depression is the discovery of homosexual inclinations. Homosexual feelings in adolescence are no guide to ultimate sexual orientation and not all adolescents who experience them continue as homosexuals in their adult life. But this knowledge does not eliminate the real suffering experienced by those who have to make sense of, and come to terms with, their feelings. Occasionally these feelings are clear-cut and precise as both the daily reality and the unconscious world of dreams show clearly that homosexuality and not heterosexuality is the basis of sexual attraction. More often, the situation is far from being clear-cut and mixed feelings exist. The exploration and understanding of the adolescent's feelings, the informing of parents and coming to terms with this situation can be accompanied by marked depression.

Here is a highly intelligent man who entertained a fear of being homosexual (with no good reason in fact) describing his feelings of returning home from a visit to some friends in the country. He had no idea he was deeply depressed and some time later wrote this account of the fears that were haunting him at the time.

I sat there thinking, feeling and not relating to anyone else. Everyone else was ignored and all feelings inside me had to be acted out, felt solely within myself. I thought about the awful week and thoughts seemed to come pouring out. The week had been so bad that I suppose it was inevitable that I should assume they must have discovered my secret. For some time now I had decided that something was odd, queer, homosexual about me. I had been trying to hide the secret for three years and yet all the time I seemed to be looking over my shoulder to see whether people were looking at me because of my odd reactions.

But could the secret have been found out? Had I done anything during my visit which could be interpreted the wrong way round? My mind went round and round. Oh, Lord, it stood out a mile. Which is the most obvious sign to the outside world of homosexuality? Obviously kissing another man. John, my host, had done just that when I arrived and left. My secret is out; they must have realized it; they all saw it in my mind.

Three years' efforts had been to no avail. But if they know now they may have known before and so my mind began racing back to see which other things would show that they knew all along. There was the occasion at the garage when John had shown complete contempt for me; yes, complete contempt and yet I pretended that he was not rejecting me. Now I could see it and accept it. There was the strange episode when we were going for a drink at the pub. He walked up to the bar, slammed a glass down, grabbed the bottle of whisky and poured some in the glass only to turn suddenly on his heels and go out. Why? Now I know.

My mind raced back through these and other events which confirmed my suspicions that my secret was known.

Any previous justifications for my continued existence had gone – it was just a matter of time now. I looked about me and I knew it, so must they. I got up, I could not sit amongst the other people any longer. Something had kept me going until now; I felt now that I had to die. I would go back home and there die. There was nothing more to do.

The feeling of being found out in fact led to a serious suicidal attempt and it was only later that the incapacitating, damaging impact of the depressive state with its falsifying effect became clear.

(c) *Work*. Sexual experiences are part of our innermost world and our struggles and joys are intensely personal. Work, on the other hand, is something that cannot be hidden. It is either done or not, brings satisfaction or boredom and provokes comment from others, notably those for whom this activity is visible evidence of responsibility, industry and achievement. For a smaller proportion of the population there is no sharp transition between school and work, through the intervention of College and University. For the overwhelming majority, school-leaving means starting work and financial independence. For many the nature of the work does not present a problem, but for some it does.

A common problem is the adolescent's uncertainty about what work he or she would like to do. They are expected to know, but many do not, and so feel embarrassed and frustrated by their own growing confusion. This situation can breed intense unhappiness and the victim can easily become depressed. Family and society expect them to work and, if they do not, they are considered lazy and irresponsible. It takes courage to stand up to such social disapproval.

So they carry on working, doing something they hate and yet are unable to find any alternative that suits them.

Erikson has chosen George Bernard Shaw's autobiographical comments to illustrate this aspect of identity confusion in adolescence:

> The truth is that all men are in a false position in society until they have realized their possibilities and imposed them on their neighbours. They are tormented by a continual shortcoming in themselves; yet they irritate others by a continual overweening. This discord can be resolved by acknowledged success or failures; everyone is ill at ease until he has found his natural place, whether it is above or below his birth place.[15]

At the age of twenty, stuck in an office, Shaw was clearly acutely unhappy, particularly as he realized that he was doing his work well and that he had the mark of success.

> I made good in spite of myself and found, to my dismay, that Business, instead of expelling me as the worthless impostor I was, was fastening upon me with no intention of letting go. Behold me, therefore, in my twentieth year, with a business training, in an occupation which I detested as cordially as any sane person lets himself detest anything he cannot escape from. In March 1876 I broke loose.[16]

Shaw, however, had enough self-awareness and self-discipline to start the profession which made him famous.

> My office training had left me with a habit of doing something regularly each day as a fundamental condition of industry as distinguished from idleness. I knew I was making no headway unless I was doing this, and that I should never produce a book in any other fashion. I bought supplies of white paper, demy size, by sixpence-worths at a time, folded it in quarto and condemned myself to fill five pages of it a day, rain or shine, dull or inspired. I had so much of the schoolboy and the clerk still in me that, if my five pages ended in the middle of a

sentence, I did not finish it until next day. On the other hand, if I missed a day, I made up for it by doing a double task on the morrow. On this plan I produced five novels in five years.[17]

Few emerge from their work crisis with the outstanding success of a Shaw. Many linger on and succumb to a level of disgruntled adaptation: but others become intensely upset, depressed, and give up work altogether. They may join others in groups to which society has given the pejorative description of drop-outs. Such men and women come from a wide assortment of backgrounds, which include those who do not know what they wish to do, those who cannot tolerate any form of restriction or authority, those who genuinely believe that the political and economic system is wrong and those who are too anxious and frightened to face their fellow human beings in the process of work. Anxiety, fear and depression are often lurking in the background and occasionally, when such young people open up and freely discuss their feelings, their inner sense of emptiness is vividly disclosed.

In Arthur Miller's *Death of a Salesman*, Biff says: 'I just can't take hold, Mum. I can't take hold of some kind of a life.'

The inability to take hold of some kind of a life is ultimately most fully portrayed when the young man or woman cannot work or leave home. Utterly paralysed, these youngsters are unable to make the minimum physical, social and emotional effort that leaving home would require. They are prisoners of their own acute fears and express a virulent form of separation anxiety. They know they should try and become independent of their families and yet they feel incapable of taking such a step. Depression is often a prominent accompaniment of such a predicament.

The home situation is often extremely complicated. The adolescent is being pushed inexorably by the process of growth and maturation towards separate independence and yet is too frightened to face it, nor can he or she acknowledge this fear. As youth is a time when there should be no fear, its admission is intensely humiliating. In such a situation there is marked pent-up frustration, feelings of anger and hostility and the need for scapegoats. Blame is either attached to the parents or to the prevailing evils of society. Whatever genuine social evils may exist, the onslaught on them will not make the slightest difference to such an adolescent who, unable to find the minimum of personal identity, is screaming at everybody else except himself. Parents, stretched beyond endurance, retaliate and scenes of violent exchanges, tears, recriminations and severe depression with suicidal attempts can and do occur.

Other home situations might involve the attempts of scared youngsters to establish their autonomy in the face of anxious parents whose fussiness hides their own dread about the safety of their children in the wide world. What is often portrayed as the fight between suppressed adolescents and authoritarian, repressive parents is often nowadays the blind, unconscious collusion of two groups of human beings frightened to let go of each other and to explore life alone.

Such fear may occasionally develop into refusal to go to school, itself an expression of the anxiety and accompanying depressive feelings resulting from worries about leaving the security of home and parents.

Marked and intense depression in adolescence is often the outward appearance of an inner fragility, or identity confusion, and the suicidal gestures are often a cry for help to rescue the person from the blind alley in which they find themselves.

Notes

1. Balkwin, H., (1972), 'Depression—A mood disorder in children and adolescents', *Maryland State Medical Journal*, Vol. 21, No. 6, pp. 55-61
2. Spitz, R. A., (1946), 'Anaclitic Depression', *Psychoanalytic Study of the Child*, 2: 312-42, Hogarth Press, London
3. Burlingham, D. and Freud, A., (1942), *Young Children in Wartime*, George Allen and Unwin, London

4. Burlingham, D. and Freud, A., (1944), *Infants Without Families,* George Allen and Unwin, London

5. Walk, A., (1964), 'The prehistory of child psychiatry', *British Journal of Psychiatry,* 110, 754

6. Frommer, E. A., (1968), 'Depressive Illness in Childhood' in *Recent Developments in Affective Disorders* ed. Coppen, A. and Walk, A., RMPA

7. Lourie, R. S., (1957), 'Suicides and attempted suicides in children and adolescents', *Texas Medicine,* 63:58

8. Otto, U., (1972), 'Suicide Acts by children and adolescents', *Acta Psychiatrica Scandinavica,* Supplement 233

9. Schaffer, D., (1974), *Journal of Child Psychology and Psychiatry and Allied Discipline,* 15:275

10. *Ibid.*

11. Connell, P. H., (1965), 'Suicidal attempts in childhood and adolescence' in *Modern Perspectives in Child Psychiatry,* Ed. Howell, S. J. G., Oliver and Boyd, Edinburgh

12. Balkwin, H., *op. cit.*

13. Johnson, P. E., (1959), *Psychology of Religion,* Abingdon Press, New York

14. Erikson, E. H., (1968), *Identity,* Faber and Faber, London

15. Shaw, G. B., (1953), *Selected Prose,* Constable, London, p. 35

16. *Ibid.,* p. 53

17. *Ibid.,* p. 58

VIII   Female Sexuality

The start of a girl's monthly period, menstruation, is one of the most conspicuous aspects of her puberty and adolescence. In all studies of depression it has been shown conclusively that, although both sexes suffer from this illness, women are far more likely to succumb to emotional disturbance, particularly depression. One of the contributing reasons for this is the intimate relationship between menstruation, childbearing, the post puerperium, and depressive reactions, which will be considered in this and the next chapter.

PREMENSTRUAL SYNDROME

If for some women the 'curse' is actual menstruation, for others it is in fact the period immediately preceding menstruation, whose arrival relieves the prior symptoms. Nowadays these symptoms have come to be known as the premenstrual syndrome and have drawn much attention from various medical studies. Physicians of the Hippocratic School had already noted the symptoms.[1] Around 100 AD Soranus of Ephesus wrote: 'The menses are about to occur when a woman feels somewhat uneasy on walking, when a feeling of heaviness appears in the loins. Some develop a torpor, yawning and pandiculation, while others develop nausea and a loss of appetite.'[2]

A shortened modern version of what happens was first considered in detail in 1931[3] and the following is a later account published in 1953:

It consists of nervous tension, irritability, anxiety, depression, bloated feelings of the abdomen, swelling of fingers and legs, tightness and itching of the skin, headaches, dizziness and palpitations. Less commonly there occurs hypersomnia, excessive thirst and appetite, increased sex desire and, in some affected subjects, an increased tendency for asthma, migraine, vasomotor rhinitis, urticaria and epilepsy.[4]

With the addition of swelling of the breasts, this is a picture which many women will recognize even though they may only experience some of the symptoms.

These symptoms usually begin two to twelve days before the period, ending, for the majority, with the beginning of menstruation. Many women have only some of these symptoms but studies have shown that the number who are severely troubled by them may vary from 20-40 per cent[5][6] of otherwise healthy women in the population.

In a few women the depressive mood is overwhelmingly strong and for some days before menstruation they are severely debilitated with the whole range of depressive manifestations including deep misery, tears, loss of energy, apathy, irritation, tension and a tendency to argumentation and quarrelling.

Such a widespread and recurrent manifestation can be expected to have an impact on other aspects of life, as was shown in a series of studies by Dr Dalton. Her studies show, among other things, that half the acute admissions to hospital, 46 per cent of acute psychiatric admissions and 50 per cent of women admitted following accidents occurred in the premenstrual period or just at menstruation. As well as this, schoolwork of girls tended to suffer in this period and crimes committed by female prisoners often occurred at about this time. 45 per cent of women reporting sick in a factory did so between one and three days prior to menstruation or when menstruating.[7] Some of the absenteeism during actual menstruation could be accounted for by painful periods.

Another serious aspect of the premenstrual syndrome is the presence of depression and its association with attempted suicide and suicide both of which have been found to occur more commonly in this phase of the cycle.[8][9]

There is no satisfactory explanation to date for this common condition but changes in the sexual hormones, particularly the oestrogen-progesterone balance, water retention as well as psychological theories have been put forward.[10]

CONTRACEPTIVE PILL

The theory linking this syndrome with the female hormones also links it with those forms of contraceptive pill which contain a mixture of oestrogens and progesterone. One prominent feature of the premenstrual syndrome is the change in mood with a decisive shift towards depression. Now one of the possible side effects of the contraceptive pill is precisely this tendency towards mood changes which include depression, but the story is not as straightforward as this because in some women the contraceptive pill actually relieves some of the premenstrual symptoms.

In one study, 152 women (attending six Family Planning Association Clinics) who were starting on an oral contraceptive pill containing an oestrogen-progesterone combination, were compared with 40 who were using mechanical means. The pill was shown to have significantly alleviated premenstrual depression, irritability and dysmenorrhoea (painful menstruation) when compared to those who used mechanical forms of birth control. On the other hand, after eleven months 20.4 per cent of women had stopped taking the pill for one or several of the following reasons: depression and irritability, 9; headaches, 13; loss of interest in sex, 6; swelling of hands and feet, 6; unacceptable weight gain, 11; very tired, 5; planning pregnancy (only reason), 5.

Depression appearing for the first time, or existing tendencies becoming much worse, occurred in 6 per cent of the women on the pill compared to 2 per cent on alternative contraceptives.[11] Thus there is some evidence that a very small but persistent percentage of women on this type of contraceptive pill either get depressed or have their tendency towards depression exaggerated to the point that they cannot use the pill.

The characteristic form of this type of depression involves pessimism, anxiety, dissatisfaction, lethargy, loss of sexual desire and the tendency to cry easily. Recent studies have shed light on one possible reason for this form of depression. In Chapter III a description was given of biochemical studies which implicated brain amine metabolism showing that there were low levels of the 5-hydroxytryptamine. Now one of the precursors of the substance (5H.T.) is L-tryptophan which is an aminoacid. Research has shown that 80 per cent of women taking oral contraceptives have some changes of tryptophan metabolism.[12] It is possible that for a very tiny number of women their depression may be linked with this biochemical change which does not have any effect on the overwhelming majority of women taking various forms of the pill.

These findings are important, not only because they show that depression in a very small number of women may have a genuine physical basis which cannot be ignored. It is also an additional support for the theory linking depressive mood changes with brain amines. It is in this strange way that science progresses, finding meaningful links from the most disparate sources.

These studies are beginning to show links which may account for the depressive reaction in some women who take the pill. It must not be forgotten, however, that the overwhelming majority do not have such a reaction, nor that other non-physical factors such as fear or a negative attitude to contraception itself may play a part which is poorly understood so far.

LIBIDO

The reduction of sexual desire or libido is a feature which is seen regularly only in the severe or endogenous form of depression. This reduction can be total, with the person having no sexual drive at all. It is a loss which is in keeping with the reduction of other instinctual drives such as appetite, which may lessen appreciably. Unless the person recognizes this loss as part of the depressed state, it may cause a great deal of worry, if not to them, then certainly to their spouse who may need enlightening as to the true cause of the apparent sexual indifference. Women sometimes go through agonies regarding the faithfulness of their husband when it is in fact his depressive state that accounts for his loss of sexual drive (which almost invariably returns when the illness is over).

The confusion can take a complicated turn in those instances where the severely depressed person begins to experience delusions of guilt regarding real or imaginary sexual misdemeanours of the past. When the depressive process is clearly understood by their spouse or relatives these 'confessions' can be placed in their proper context, although even then they can stir up unnecessary concern and pain. If the depression is not recognized, these sudden revelations can cause serious marital upheaval. The husband will describe in detail flirtations and affairs or episodes when venereal disease was contracted, even believing that he is still infected. All this may be wholly imaginary, or it may have some basis in truth which has long since ceased to play any part in the life of the individual or the couple. The wife likewise may entertain similar delusions of sexual infidelity. These delusions and mistaken beliefs are put in their true perspective by the patient after recovery and eventually they are completely forgotten.

While sexual activity undoubtedly suffers in severe depression, for some men and women the reverse is true. A mood of depression of lesser severity can be combated through sexual intercourse itself, as described in the following uninhibited description.

> I feel at times in a terrible state . . . I feel fed up, depressed . . . I feel lost . . . I don't know what to do with myself . . . When I get up in the morning I say: 'Oh, hell . . it is that bloody job.' I force myself. When I feel depressed I want to go to a room and say: 'Blast everybody.' It is not that I don't want to work . . . I do but I have to get over it . . . I have discovered that sex is a good substitute for tablets. Sex is relaxing, it helps.

Notes

1. Ricci, J. V., (1950), *The Genealogy of Gynaecology*, Blakiston, Philadelphia; p. 54
2. *Ibid.*, p. 117
3. Frank, R. T., (1931), Archives of *Neurology and Psychiatry*, 26, 1053, Chicago
4. Rees, L., (1953), *Journal of Mental Science*, 99, 62
5. *Ibid.*
6. Sutherland, H. and Stewart, I., (1965), *Lancet*, 1, 1180
7. Dalton, K., (1964), *The Premenstrual Syndrome*, Heinemann, London
8. Mackinnon, I. L., Mackinnon, P. C. B., Thompson, A. D., (1959), *British Medical Journal* I: 1015
9. Tonks, C. M., Rack, P. H., Rose, M. J., (1968), *Journal of Psychological Research*, 11, 319
10. Tonks, C. M., (1968), 'Premenstrual Tension', *British Journal of Hospital Medicine*, Vol. 1, No. 3
11. Herzberg, B., Coppen, A., (1970), 'Changes in Psychological Symptoms in Women taking Oral Contraceptives', *British Journal of Psychiatry*, 116: 161
12. Adams, P. W., Rose, D. P., Folkard J., Wynn, V., Seed, M., Strong, R., (1973), 'Effect of Pyridoxine Hydrochloride (Vit B6) upon depression associated with contraception', *Lancet* 1, 897

IX   Marriage and Childbearing

What is the relationship between marriage and childbearing and the two principal severe mental illnesses, depression and schizophrenia?

There is considerable evidence suggesting that schizophrenics marry less often than the rest of the population before their first admission to hospital and that this situation continues after discharge. However, this does not seem to be the case with depressive disorders.

A recent study in England tends to confirm these findings in the case of women. As far as schizophrenia is concerned, when schizophrenic women were compared to non-schizophrenic normal women in the population their probability of marriage was three-quarters of the normal group before illness and one-third afterwards. Women suffering from depression showed no difference in marriage rates before and after their first admission to hospital.[1] These findings refer to depression which is severe enough to require hospitalization. There is no evidence that depression, in any reduced form of severity, contributes to a lower rate of marriage.

Similarly, there is no evidence to suggest that the fertility of women suffering from depression was any different as a whole from the rest of the population. These facts refer to marriage itself. Other studies have looked exclusively at the appearance of depression during childbearing and the period after birth, technically called the post puerperium.

For the overwhelming majority of women pregnancy and childbearing is a happy experience. Obviously for a variety of reasons there are exceptions to this rule. The advent of more liberal abortion laws in this country and others has unleashed an extensive and controversial debate about the ethical considerations of the Abortion Act itself.

Clearly the circumstances surrounding the initiation or termination of life should carry the deepest considerations and the dialogue is vital for the values that any civilized society wishes to pursue. However, a basic distinction has to be made between the features themselves, social or medical, which are experienced by the woman and prompt her to seek relief in the form of abortion and abortion itself as the appropriate response to such adversity. There will always be arguments as to whether abortion is ethically correct or not and both sides argue with equal passion. Both groups, however, need to appreciate the exact nature of the symptoms that induce the seeking of abortion.

In 1971 there were about a million pregnancies in the UK, out of which over 100,000 were aborted. There is widespread agreement, from available studies, that the majority of these abortions are carried out under Clause 2 of the Abortion Act, which states:

> The continuance of the pregnancy would involve risk of injury to the physical or mental health of the pregnant woman greater than if the pregnancy were terminated.

It is also generally agreed that when health is considered as the ground for termination it is, as often as not, mental rather than physical health that is at stake. This means that there is a substantial number of women suffering sufficiently from depression to be given an abortion. Their depressions usually carry the marks of reactivity, that is to say depression and anxiety are the prominent features.

Thus depression may arise because the pregnancy is out of wedlock, or the father is not interested, or it was an accident, or it was unplanned within the marriage, or it was a contraceptive failure, or the required family size was already achieved, or the previous pregnancies left a trail of distress or the woman just simply did not want to have a baby. In a few instances the woman has been raped. These and many other reasons lead to an increasingly growing feeling of marked despondency, fear, tension, disturbed sleep, worry, loss of appetite, reduced concentration, irritability, inability to carry on with normal activities, weeping, tension and emotional outbursts. Such women will complain of feeling 'terrible', 'awful', 'horrible', sometimes 'desperate', of 'life not being worth living', that they 'can't go on'.

When one realizes that 12 to 15 per cent of all pregnancies end in abortion, one can see that women presenting these features make up a substantial proportion of human beings whose suffering is intensive and expresses itself often through a depressive picture. Now it is known from available studies that a high proportion of these women have what psychiatry describes as a neurotic predisposition, which is found equally in a similar high proportion of those suffering from the pre-menstrual syndrome.[2]

The high incidence of neurotic characteristics in these two groups of women raises acute medical and moral issues which are worth discussing. The word neurotic in a lay sense has often a pejorative descriptive quality which is equivalent to being a second-class citizen. No exact description of this second-rate quality exists but it implies that the woman fusses a lot, exaggerates, often becomes overtly weepy, raises her voice to shout or scream, causes a scene which has an exaggerated, dramatic note about it, lacks control and therefore appears to be childish or attention seeking. These characteristics of emotional lability, marked exhibitions of distress and possible suicidal threats appear to some people as a storm in a tea-cup and the person is generally termed 'hysterical'.

The word hysterical as used by the medical profession has a whole variety of meanings, all of which indicate psychological causes of symptoms as opposed to physical. A naïve interpretation of the word might indicate that one group of symptoms is genuine (the physical) and the other unreal or fabricated. This distinction between the pseudo and the genuine causes endless controversy in many aspects of the practice of medicine. It is sufficient to note here that neurotic symptoms are, in the majority of instances, genuine, be they physical or psychological in character. The person is really experiencing the distress even if the cause is not clearly physical in origin. Thus to dismiss the state as neurotic, hysterical and by implication treat the suffering as simply an unwarranted exaggeration of little consequence does not do justice to the person.

People with a neurotic disposition are as talented, gifted intelligent as the rest of the population, if not more so. They happen as a group to have a greater tendency towards the experiences and manifestation of certain characteristics such as anxiety, mood swings, low threshold to pain and a sensitivity to stress which they experience more easily and to a greater degree than others. To dismiss their suffering or distress as fake, or to pass adverse opinions on their behaviour is an unwarranted moral judgment without any factual foundation. Equally, on the other hand, a society or those with certain religious beliefs have a right to insist that the way to cope with suffering is not always to eliminate it, that there are higher values which demand the acceptance of suffering, (i.e. from an unwanted pregnancy) rather than its elimination and that the law should reflect this value.

Although the controversy round abortion centres principally on the freedom of the individual and the right to exercise this freedom without fear or punishment, ultimately this – as so many other controversial issues – reflects the individual's response to suffering. Suffering is ultimately a personal choice and any decisions the individual makes are bound to be influenced by his or her own values and priorities.

As the law stands in Great Britain at present there are few reasons, other than those of conscience, for denying an abortion to a woman who expresses marked feelings of depression and anxiety as described above and many terminations are carried out on these grounds.

There have been few follow-up studies after termination or when termination has been refused. One of the most detailed was carried out in Sweden on 479 women who were aborted on psychiatric grounds. In a follow-up study of 2-3 years afterwards it was found that some 14 per cent felt mild self-reproach and 11 per cent serious self-reproach. These 11 per cent of women had also unpleasant sequels in which they felt decisively depressed. However, this depression was not severe enough to impair working capacity.[3]

A more recent study in Britain shows far more favourable results.[4] Of 120 patients terminated on psychiatric recommendation the family doctor considered at a follow-up six months later that 70 patients had improved, 23 initially improved but then remained unchanged; 11 were unchanged;

6 were temporarily worse and only one was certainly worse, with 9 unknown.

Quite clearly, abortion is not an easy answer to the problems of depression in the presence of an unwanted pregnancy. A good deal more research is needed to clarify the possible results of abortions which, in a few people, include a severe exacerbation of the depressive symptoms. The overwhelming majority either benefit or certainly do not deteriorate in the short term from such an operation. But such abrupt and basic interventions in the process of life need a good deal more information than we have at present to assess the long term significance to the personality. This does not exist and, until research is carried out satisfactorily, the subject will remain controversial. Indeed, one suspects that no study will ever put an end to such a controversial subject as it involves questions which are both practical and spiritual in nature.

If the abortion is refused will there be an inevitable deterioration: what are the risks of suicide – which, articulated or not, is frequently in the background of desperation?

Another piece of research, carried out in Sweden, examined these questions in a follow-up study of 249 women whose applications for an abortion were refused.[5] 86 per cent continued the pregnancy and had the child, 3 per cent had a spontaneous miscarriage, 11 per cent procured an abortion illegally. Although only 11 per cent had an abortion illegally, 30 per cent had planned to try and a total of 18 per cent actually tried. Despite the mixture of feelings, 73 women were ultimately content with these decisions but emphasized the wide variety of difficulties that surrounded the continuation of the pregnancy. 27 remained dissatisfied with the decision and would have preferred an abortion. In terms of their health, 76 per cent had adjusted well, but 24 per cent needed sick leave and were still displaying distress at the follow-up $7\frac{1}{2}$ years later. This was a distinctly high figure.

Such a relatively high intensity of distress would suggest the possibility of a high incidence of suicidal attempts and even suicide itself. Some 12 per cent of all the women made suicidal threats but no suicides or attempted suicides followed the rejection of the application.

In the British study mentioned above, of the 109 refusals 6 had a spontaneous miscarriage and 32 had an abortion elsewhere, which is a higher figure than the Swedish study showed. Surprisingly, of the 55 who completed their pregnancy, only 5 were worse. Once again, none committed suicide.

The absence of suicide in both these studies suggests that depression in this group of women does not carry a high risk of suicide. But this certainly is not invariable and a very small number of women who threaten suicide do in fact kill themselves.

The complexity of factors involved, in relation to the health and life of every woman in this kind of depressive situation, makes a medical evaluation one of the most difficult and painful clinical responsibilities. All but a tiny minority of women who present themselves for termination are convinced of the misery of their lives and there must be very strong evidence to the contrary to refute the patient's subjective state. Even if this exists, the only thing a psychiatrist can do with confidence is to diagnose and exclude the severe forms of depression. In fact, psychiatrists who only recognize the severe forms and dismiss the rest as neurotic reactions – which by definition the patient should be able to handle with assistance – have a simple task. For the rest there is a Herculean task which in the end comes down to the fact that an individual woman, with the few exceptions of verifiable falsification, feels genuinely depressed. It is not the task of the doctor to act as a moral adjudicator, provided he has ascertained her ethical attitude. The Abortion Act allows for termination on health grounds and so, for the time being, any woman who feels these symptoms and can find a doctor who agrees with them should, in theory, be able to have an abortion if the facilities are available. In practice this does not work in this way because many doctors have strong objections to the Act on ethical grounds and, even if these are not as absolute as Roman Catholic objections, still feel that the Abortion Act of 1967 is too permissive. Doctors' training is by nature directed towards the preservation of life, not towards its eradication.

It is thus understandable that the present situation regarding abortion is laden with confusion and difficulties involving the classification of depression, the suffering of individual women, and the dilemma of doctors who have no strong religious convictions but who worry about agreeing to an abortion which the woman may regret later on, perhaps many years later. There is also the problem of those doctors with strong religious convictions who have a double responsibility: to their conscience in preserving the sanctity of life, and to the wellbeing of their patients. None of these issues admits to an easy solution. The reader may properly consider that, while they have a good deal of sympathy with the doctor, they have equal sympathy with the woman who is the actual sufferer and who depends on the medical profession to give her the right answer.

Despite the Abortion Act, the whole question of abortion remains a highly controversial issue with much agony experienced both by the doctor, and by the patient and her relatives. One of the reasons for allocating so much room in a book on depression to this subject is to show that, in a very high proportion of cases, depressive feelings, intense misery and possibly suicidal threats are the means of communicating the woman's desperation.

PREGNANCY AND POST PUERPERIUM

PREGNANCY

For the overwhelming majority of women pregnancy does not constitute any form of threat to their wellbeing and, although these nine months may have other minor or major disadvantages, depression is usually not amongst them. Occasionally a depressive reaction may occur during pregnancy, particularly if there are other social or psychological complications, but medical assistance is not often needed. Indeed, for some patients who have experienced recurrent bouts of depression, pregnancy may give them unexpected and much appreciated relief and a sense of wellbeing.

POST PUERPERIUM

The rarity of a depressive reaction in the course of pregnancy is followed by a period immediately after birth which is well known for its depressive potential. This was noted as far back as Hippocrates who cited a case of a woman who gave birth to twins, experienced severe insomnia and restlessness on the sixth day of the postpartum, became delirious on the eleventh day, went into a coma and died on the seventeenth. Hippocrates speculated regarding the cause of postpartum mental illness, offering two hypotheses, firstly that lochial discharge, when suppressed, could be carried towards the head resulting in agitation, delirium and attacks of mania and, secondly, that 'when blood collects at the breasts of a woman, it indicates madness'. These hypotheses were treated as dogma for the next two thousand years.[6]

Many of the post puerperal illnesses continued to be related to the presence of infection and the delirium associated with it. Nowadays the presence of effective treatment has eliminated the infective element thus isolating the post puerperal depressive syndromes a little more clearly. They are divided into three groups.

'MATERNAL BLUES'

'Maternal Blues' is a condition characterized by fatigue, crying, anxiety over the baby, headaches, inability to sleep, confusion and sometimes hostility towards the husband. The incidence of this condition is extremely high and has been variously estimated from 50 to 80 per cent of all pregnancies.[7] [8]

In one study 50 per cent of women experienced maternal blues.[9] Of these 50 women, 66 per cent developed the condition within four days of parturition and 26 per cent on the third day. Most women describe tearfulness and misery lasting for a matter of hours, at most for one to three days. In some it lasts longer. The depression is accompanied by some anxiety and confusion which shows itself in poor concentration and forgetfulness.

These symptoms are so common that most women can be expected to experience them. Provided women are fore-warned they are forearmed and no action needs to be taken with very few exceptions. They do not signify any serious developments.

ATYPICAL DEPRESSION

A much smaller number of women, found in one study to be about 10 per cent of pregnancies, undergo a more complicated depressive illness at a later stage of their delivery. This can be a week or more after the birth of the baby. The author of this investigation[10] describes this group of depressions, which fit in much more with the 'reactive', 'neurotic', 'atypical' form, thus:

> The depression became evident after the return home (from hospital) as a prevailing despondency, tearfulness, feelings of inadequacy to cope (especially with the baby), fears for her own and the baby's health, tension, irritability and undue fatigue, diminished appetite, difficulty in getting to sleep and decline in sexual interest.

When the same group of patients was followed up a year later, some 4 per cent of them had not improved but con-tinued to suffer loss of sexual desire, irritability, excessive fatigue, depression and disturbed sleep.

Little attention has generally been paid to this small number of women with persistent depressive features but they have been noted as contributing significantly to marital break-down as the following account of a married couple shows.

After the wife had undergone prolonged periods of depression (which in one case lasted as long as nine years), the couple finally went to a marriage council. The immediate problem was the deteriorating relationship between husband and wife who were contemplating separation or divorce. The story was not distinguishable from the familiar pattern of accusation and counteraccusation until, either accidentally or through specific questioning, one or other spouse admitted that the problem started with the birth of the last child.

What emerged then was a classic situation. Following the birth of the child, the mother felt tired and lacked her usual energy. She became irritable and snappy with the other members of the family. This sort of behaviour may have been usual for her previously, in which case it becomes markedly more severe, or unusual and out of keeping with her character. These symptoms were explained away by the arrival of the new child with the increased load it imposed on the mother. In addition to the marked fatigue and irritability, there was a diminution of sexual desire varying from a total loss and avoidance of all sexual relations to a reluctant and non-enjoyable resumption for the sake of the husband. Everyone expected the situation to improve and in the interval the husband and the relatives gave a helping hand. But the situation did not change and, after a few months, tolerant patience gave way to marked criticism and then to open grumbling by the husband who was no longer able to recognize his wife. She was criticized on the grounds that she was not really trying and in no time at all the words 'selfish', 'irresponsible' and 'lazy' were being flung about. The wife was trying desperately all the time to emerge from this wretched state and could not. After a while the marriage began to suffer and the situation gradually deteriorated to the point where a break-up was contemplated.[11]

Some of these conditions do respond to appropriate treatment even at a late stage but the important precaution is to register the condition as an illness and to seek help from the family doctor at the earliest possible moment.

SEVERE DEPRESSION

Seeking help from the doctor and, if necessary, from the psychiatrist and through hospitalization becomes necessary for any serious mental illness that occurs in the year after the birth of the child. The two serious illnesses are schizophrenia and severe depression. Depression is the commonest form of mental illness at this time but the incidence for this severe form of mental illness is minute and is of the order of one birth in a thousand, so that it is an extremely rare event. When it does occur, the patient usually responds to the modern range of treatments such as ECT or drugs and the prospects for full recovery are excellent. A detailed follow-up study also showed that only one in five of those who suffered from such severe depression had a recurrence with the next pregnancy.[12]

The arrival of a baby confronts a woman with major physical, social and emotional changes. Her whole style of life alters and responds to these changes. Her feelings regarding her ability to care, to cope with the withdrawal from her work – at least temporarily – to adjust in her new relationship with her husband and the hormonal changes in her body all combine to provoke major stresses and readjustments. The frequency of a whole variety of depressive reactions is but one indication that what is universally considered as a 'natural thing' is, in fact, a very complicated process requiring a wide range of adjustments and adaptations.

MARRIAGE

There are no systematic observations on the relationship between marriage and depression apart from the post puerperal conditions just referred to. And yet marriage under stress provides one of the commonest sources of distress. This is clearly shown by the frequent mention of marital difficulties as a major precipitating factor in those who attempt suicide. Depression in marriage is closely related to the fluctuating stresses and ultimately to the breakdown of a relationship,[13] but some of the features need emphasizing.

First of all, a depressive reaction, usually of the 'reactive' variety, is the commonest reaction to any disruption of the one-to-one relationship or bond by the couple. The parent-child bond is the prototype of the attachment formed by a pair of human beings intimately related to one another. The husband-wife relationship resembles in many ways this primal one-to-one relationship and its disruption or threatened disruption may well lead to the same depressive sequence. This is often seen when the husband or wife faces the prospect of losing his/her partner suddenly and unexpectedly, that is to say, when up to that moment there had been no hint of marital difficulties.

A woman, aged 42, had been married for 14 years. She considered her marriage to be 'ideal'. Her husband was a businessman who up to now appeared to be devoted to her. Their sexual life was good, both enjoyed sexual intercourse two to three times a week and both felt free to respond to each other's needs. There were no children by mutual agreement but neither had any regrets.

The husband was slightly older and by nature was a quiet, shy man who spent all his spare time at home. Neither of them enjoyed parties or social gatherings, but found much pleasure in their garden, reading and music. They could share and discuss their problems and had no secrets from each other.

The wife admitted that never for a moment did it cross her mind that this contentment could be threatened. They lived in an isolated spot in the country and the nearest house was about a mile away. It changed ownership and the new occupant was a single woman, divorced and an artist. Within a year this 'happy, blissful scene' was transformed. It became abundantly clear to the wife that her husband was having – 'I don't know what to call it; an affair, a liaison. I have not asked; I don't want to know.'

The complicated reasons for this happening belong to the study of marital pathology but the wife's reaction was typical. Up to now her life had been orderly and disciplined and she took great pride in her home. Now she noticed she could concentrate less and less. Her sleep began to suffer. She would go to bed at 10, 11 or midnight and lie awake for an hour or more, waking up at 5 or 6 in the morning. She woke up tired, with a headache, and was still in her dressing-gown at mid-morning, something that had never occurred before.

She stopped cooking a midday meal and her smoking consumption went up and up. She found herself smoking 40 or 50 cigarettes a day, turning to alcohol for comfort and several times during the day bursting into tears. She became increasingly irritable and hurled abuses at her husband without wanting to do so. 'I know that I am driving him further away with these stupid remarks. They are not me at all. There are in fact two of me. This stupid, mad, weepy woman, completely out of control and the other, my normal self, I can't get hold of.' Ultimately she made a suicidal attempt which compelled the husband to look at the relationship afresh.

But the cycle of marital stress leading to a depressive reaction (rarely a manic one), which itself aggravates and intensifies the conflict by the exaggerated hostility of the hurt partner, is commonplace. It leads to another feature often reduced to these words – 'I am not mad, doctor, am I? My husband/wife says I am mad and I should be locked up.'

If the reaction to the stress is a depressive one with marked anxiety features, this often leads to exaggerated, angry, tearful, histrionic scenes which are labelled as 'mad' by the partner who, consciously or unconsciously, may find this a convenient excuse to strengthen his or her desire to leave home. For people who are threatened with the loss of their spouse, to have the added indignity of being labelled as mad or even being threatened that the children will be taken away from them because of their behaviour, the situation reaches intolerable proportions which may lead to suicidal gestures.

MARITAL BREAKDOWN

The period leading up to and following the departure of the spouse is one in which depressive reactions are extremely common. The departure of the spouse may be permanent and the one who remains behind often goes through the same sequence of protest, despair and detachment as that seen in young children when the mother departs.

Protest and despair are a mixture of depression, anger and

a sense of hopelessness which is seen again and again in these situations. The husband or wife left behind experiences the whole range of depressive manifestations with marked changes of mood, insomnia, loss of energy, irritability, weight loss, lack of concentration, loss of interest in living and apathy. If the departure is irreversible, a period of detachment follows and most people find their equanimity months later.

Unfortunately the process is never as tidy as this. Those who intend to leave may take a long time to make up their minds and there may be a protracted period when hope is rekindled only to be dashed again. The go-return-go relationship is reflected in the emotions and makes heavy inroads in the affective life of the individual. Even when the final departure is complete, contact may be resumed when children are visited and when divorce proceedings commence. All these encounters may reawaken the depressive reaction. The degree of despair may be marked; a little-known fact about suicide is that the period between breakdown and the reconstruction of a new relationship carries an enormous threat to life.[14]

Notes

1. Stevens, B. C., (1969), 'Marriage and Fertility of Women suffering from Schizophrenia or Affected Disorders', Maudsley Monograph, 19, Oxford University Press
2. Coppen, A., (1965), British Journal of Psychiatry, 111:115
3. Ekblad, M., (1956), 'Induced Abortion on Psychiatric Grounds', Acta Psychiatrica Scandinavica, Supplement 99
4. Clark, M., Forstner, I., Pond, D. A., Tredgold, R. F., (1968), 'Sequels of Unwanted Pregnancy', Lancelot, 2, 501
5. Hook, K., (1963), 'Refused Abortion Act', Acta Scandinavica Psychiatrica, Supplement 168
6. Hamilton, J. A., (1962), Post Psychiatric Problems, Mosby, St Louis, p. 126
7. Pitt, B., (1973), 'Maternity Blues', British Journal of Psychiatry, 122, 431
8. Robin, A. M., (1962), 'Psychological changes in normal parturition', Psychiatric Quarterly, 36, 129

9. Pitt, B., *op. cit.*
10. Pitt, B., (1968), 'Psychiatric Illness following Childbirth', *Hospital Medicine*, April, p. 815
11. Dominian, J., (1968), *Marital Breakdown*, Pelican, Harmondsworth, p. 115
12. Martin, M. E., (1958), 'Puerperal, Mental Illness: a follow-up study of 75 cases', *British Medical Journal* II, 773
13. Dominian, J., *op. cit.*
14. Barraclough, B. M., (1971), *Personal Communication*

X Middle Age

Marriage poses specific problems in the middle years, some of which may contribute to depression. When discussing middle age there are no sharp lines of demarcation, physical or social in character, such as – for example – the onset of puberty and menstruation in girls or the school leaving age for both sexes.

Adolescence, with its three crucial characteristics of separation from home, the initiation of work and the establishment of sexual relationships, forms three identifiable crisis points which demand successful negotiations if sustained tension and a depressive response is to be avoided.

The middle years create an entirely different set of problems. Women's capacity to bear children ceases. The family also goes through a phase in which parents have to respond to the challenge of their children's adolescence followed by an extended period in which marriage returns to an exclusive relationship of the spouses, following the departure of the children from home. Finally, work assumes special significance because these should be the years of the highest achievement.

These three phenomena will be considered from the point of view of the psychological stress which they can generate which, in some instances, is severe enough to trigger off a depressive reaction. The assumption that stress arising from these conflicts can precipitate depressive states is based both on widespread clinical observation and recent research which relates stress of the life cycle to the precipitation of depressive illness.

We are assuming, of course, that (biological features apart) the challenges of middle age are faced only after the challenges of our childhood and youth have already been successfully dealt with. However, there is a small number of men and women who enter their fortieth year without having settled down to any gratifying or stable employment, have still not established rapport sexually with the opposite sex, or their own sex in the case of homosexuals, or are single but have not come to terms with their way of life.

At work they have drifted from job to job, never staying for more than a short period. The basis of such instability is accounted for by repeated dismissals or voluntary resignations with periods of unemployment in between. Their superiors are considered authoritarian, insensitive, demanding, bullying or are supposed to have a grudge against them. While this occasionally might be correct, it is unlikely to happen in successive jobs and is far more likely to reflect the sensitivity of the individual.

Others are convinced that their intelligence is not fully used and have totally unrealistic expectations, expecting to qualify for tasks which demand skills, which they can convince no one but themselves that they possess. Occasionally they will start businesses of their own which are repeatedly unsuccessful, losing their own money and that of their relatives, friends and others.

Throughout their twenties and thirties all these failures can be rationalized in one form or another. They have been unlucky, their next job will be *the one,* no one appreciates their true merits. Occasionally success finally rewards their efforts but, for the rest, the day of reckoning arrives sooner or later. The advent of the forties no longer permits the daydreaming or self-deception to continue and a sense of failure may suddenly erupt and destroy the carefully built illusionary world. Confrontation with the truth or, at most, part of the truth may have a drastic effect and a full-blown depressive reaction can result.

Similarly, depressive reactions may follow repeated failures to establish satisfactory sexual relationships. Earlier disappointments could be explained in one of several forms. 'There is plenty of time.' 'Work comes first.' 'Work is so satisfying that there is no time for anything else' or duty to parents. 'Men only want one thing.' 'Women are after your money.' 'I am used to my ways.' These and similar explanations may, in fact, remain the true convictions of some of these claimants and they continue their single state based on these beliefs. Others know in their heart of hearts that this is a form of whistling in the dark but learn to accept and adapt successfully. But for those who reach their late thirties or, indeed their forties, and have still not come to recognize clearly the nature of their particular difficulty, the arrival of the fifth decade can produce a gradual or sudden psychological shock which begins with a depressive state.

In all these instances men and women in the second half of life are still negotiating the challenges of the first half. Depressions, heavy drinking, sometimes gambling, excessive preoccupation with appearance and physical health are the frantic responses to this crisis. Sometimes the death of one or both parents is not only a source of intense grief but removes the last remaining reason which explains satisfactorily, at least to themselves, their predicament. The parental loss compels them to reassess their situation and to discover themselves. Such a combination of loss and self-discovery may prove overwhelming, destroying the lifelong protective structure they have built around themselves.

Nevertheless the majority of the single population of this age group have come to terms with their state and a combination of work, friends, social interest, and faith is enough to protect them from a depressive reaction.

Returning to the specific challenges of middle age, three features will be considered; namely work, menopause and marriage.

WORK

In a series of interviews[1] carried out within a particular company, the following remarks were made by male employees aspiring to top management.

> I am thirty-seven now. If I am going to get into management I've got to be there by forty. The company is starting to retire people at fifty-five.

> When you're forty you're an old man in this company.

At forty I can't find another job in my own line without going down a grade.

People going to the top reach management level by thirty-five to forty.

If one's not made it by forty one's had it. Also one has less energy.

These remarks reflect typically the anxieties of men approaching this period and the facts closely correspond to these views. In a study[2] of promotion patterns of 547 foremen, it was found that fewer than one in five had reached foreman status after the age of forty-five and one in ten after the age of fifty. The average age at promotion to departmental manager was 40.4 years and three-quarters attained promotion between thirty and forty.

The quotations and the research findings are from separate studies, both emphasizing a reality that exists in the minds of those who are seeking this type of promotion.

In adolescence work establishes a vital stake in the claim of adulthood. Thereafter it continues to provide a powerful pillar in the construction of the self-image; the personal identity and its fluctuating course contributes an indispensable part in the total sense of wellbeing. Freud considered that the basic requirements of human existence were to be found in love and work.[3]

There are three types of work crises met regularly in middle age. The first involves most commonly the man, (rarely the woman) who has been bypassed for a crucial promotion and now knows that, unless something exceptional occurs, he has reached the zenith of his acknowledged competence and achievement. The majority of us have a shrewd suspicion of our own capabilities and the disappointment does not come as a stunning surprise, provided we consider that the selection was fair. But for a few who secretly entertain inflated assessments of themselves their failure is a heavy blow to their hopes. Similar disappointment is experienced with the rejection of ideas or plans. These frustrations become doubly painful when those promoted are younger and can wield authority and power over an older person.

The second crisis is much rarer and is the reverse of the first group. Here a person has actually attained his promotion only to find that the fulfilment of his life's ambition is accompanied by a feeling of being stretched beyond his capacity. As depression descends, his strained resources suffer further and he is filled with doubt and questioning regarding his abilities. He begins to question seriously the wisdom of holding his post and, at the height of his depressive state, may decide to tender his resignation.

Success may be associated with yet another form of depression. Occasionally the person who has spent all his working life trying to reach a particular goal, does so at the expense of the family and other interests. Having done so, he realizes his inner emptiness, his lack of contact with the members of his family and discovers that he has no other subject or topic of interest. In a sense, he feels he has to start life all over again without the possibilities or opportunities of youth.

The third and most disturbing situation is the loss of work. In recent years, with unemployment hitting all grades of work, many men at all levels — including the executive grade — find themselves suddenly out of work, which occasionally causes a fairly severe depression characterized by feelings of misery and apathy, tension, irritation, broken sleep, smoking and drinking excessively. Pent-up feelings of anger may be intimately linked with the depressive state.

These work crises, which are difficult enough in themselves, become a nightmare if the failure at work is followed up by criticism and resentment at home. This, of course, is very likely to occur in the presence of marked marital trouble.

MARITAL STRESS

Published statistics show that 75 per cent of all marital breakdown occurs in the first twenty years of marriage[4] which means that most of it will have occurred prior to the period under consideration.

Frequently in this age group the crisis occurs in a family in which the husband has been a distant figure, aloof and preoccupied with his own interests. The mother has coped with the tasks of childbearing until the children reach adolescence, when two things occur. First the adolescents enter the inevitable phase of separation which so often requires some form of resistance and rebellion to parental authority. All the familiar exchanges of rudeness, disobedience and defiance increase and the mother finds the task beyond her. As a result the father is called upon to assist in the task of disciplining.

A father who has had little involvement with the children for a long period finds it exceedingly difficult to gain their confidence in a short time and to act as a source of respected authority. The adolescents resent such intervention and ignore it, in which case the anxiety of mother rises and the conflicts between the parents escalate. Father is suddenly expected to give sexual counselling, get involved with sons regarding their career, lay down firm principles about times of return from parties and dances and act as an effective deterrent against smoking, drugs and unacceptable sexual behaviour. Sometimes sustained efforts actually manage to succeed; often the task proves beyond him.

In any case a combination of open rebellion by the adolescents, with direct involvement in drugs, delinquency or pregnancy, coupled with open conflict between the parents who are blaming each other, produces an atmosphere of such tension that the only escape may be to succumb to a depressive illness. Prior to it there is often an increase in anxiety and, when the consumption of tranquillizing drugs prescribed by the doctor does not sufficiently improve the symptoms, then a depressive illness may supervene.

When the children have left home, one by one, there follows in these particular marriages a realization in which the couple recognize that their marriage had really existed in and through the children who gave them both a reason – however limited for the father – to sustain the union. Their departure confronts the parents with an emptiness, a lack of communication which, in fact, has existed for many years but was camouflaged by the demands of childrearing.

Even now the vacuum can be filled by the wife going out to work, which in any case often happens, even in the overwhelming majority of normal marriages. But sometimes this cannot occur and it is the wife who succumbs to a severe depressive illness requiring hospitalization. In these instances she feels totally unqualified, untrained for any work and is afraid to leave home and explore the possibility of work.

Of course the majority of couples experience an inevitable degree of emptiness when their children leave, which is a form of severance of bonding, but generally welcome their newly discovered freedom and their release from further responsibilities. The freedom is of particular importance in the case of the wife who needs a boost of confidence in tackling the new situation. Most women achieve just this but a few respond with gloom and despondency and lean heavily on their spouses for support. This demands an ability on the part of the husband to draw closer to his wife and provide the necessary comfort.

SEXUAL ACTIVITY

Some of this comfort will be found in and through their sexual life and here there will be an additional strain for the wife if she is experiencing a prolonged and distressing menopause. Menstruation most commonly stops at about the age of fifty but the production of hormones from the ovaries has been waning some time before that. It should be remembered that at the turn of the century life expectation was about fifty years, so that the phenomenon of prolonged survival with many women experiencing marked post-menopausal manifestations is a recent historical event.

Hot flushes, sweating, palpitations and psychological disturbances with depression as a prominent feature are not uncommon at the menopause, although they are far from being inevitable. It is the combination of domestic stress and marked menopausal symptoms which becomes intolerable.

Another common contribution of depression in these

years is a post-hysterectomy depression. Hysterectomy is indicated for some women for a variety of gynaecological reasons and in some women depression may follow this operation.

Depression in all these circumstances not only carries its own familiar distressing manifestations but it may severely lower the confidence of the woman in her own esteem, attractiveness and ability to be of interest to her husband. The depression can reduce sexual feelings at a time when intercourse is urgently needed for reassurance.

In fact the menopause does not by itself alter in any noticeable way sexual desire which may decrease, increase or remain unaltered. What may happen, however, in a few instances is that the anxieties of the wife are translated into a sudden increase of her sexual needs. A husband, unaccustomed to such sexual demands, may find himself impotent in the face of such sexual pressures.

IMPOTENCE

Normally there is no cause for worry since impotence in middle age is still a rarity, at least in the forties. The findings of Kinsey clearly indicate that impotence is a phenomenon associated with ageing.[5] He found that at forty the percentage of impotence is 1.9 per cent, rising to 6.7 per cent at fifty and fifty-five and only beginning to jump at sixty with a figure of 18.4 per cent.

Nevertheless, for the few who experience impotence in this age group, the prospects after a period of continual impotence over a period of three to five years is not good,[6] and the couples have to make the necessary adjustment.

Adjustment is relatively easy for such couples except when sexual intercourse is used exclusively by the man to gain reassurance for his masculinity, and by both husband and wife for the feeling of personal significance to each other. In the presence of persistent impotence wives may also get seriously upset, first fearing the arrival of another woman and, when they are reassured about this, the reason for the cessation of intercourse which they may interpret as a rejection of their sexual effectiveness.

Criticism of the husband's failure not only does not help but, indeed, may add to his deepening depression. Both partners can get very depressed by their loss of sexual contact, a misery which will only be dispelled with an explanation about the natural causes of the condition and the discovery of new ways of showing affection to each other which will compensate for their sexual loss.

The middle years show a marked increase in the incidence of depression. One reason for this is that the personal predisposition for depression (genetic and constitutional) shows itself for the first time in these years. The second is the presence of the stresses of these years which exert their own independent effect. The third is a combination of physical, psychological and social factors without the resilience of youth to combat them, making these years particularly susceptible to depressive illnesses.

Notes

1. Sofer, C., (1970), *Men in Mid-Career,* Cambridge University Press, p. 274
2. Heron, A., Chown, S. M., (1960), 'Semi-skilled and Over Forty', *Occupational Psychology,* p. 1
3. Neff, W. S., (1965), 'Psychoanalytical Concepts of the Meaning of Work', *Psychiatry,* 28
4. H.M.S.O., (1972), *Social Trends,* Table 7, 'Divorce', p. 63
5. Kinsey, A. C., *et al.,* (1948), *Sexual Behaviour in the Human Male,* Sanders, London
6. Cooper, D., (1972), 'The causes and management of Impotence', *Postgraduate Medical Journal,* 48, 548

XI Death and Mourning

As we reach and pass middle age we increasingly have to cope with death, a fact everyone is aware of but gives little anticipatory consideration to until a loss occurs in the family. Two features are specially worthy of notice, namely the range of expectation of life and the sex distribution of age at death.

TABLE III

Expectation of Life at Birth (Modified)

	1841	*1901–1910*	*1930–1932*	*1969*
Men	40·2	48·5	58·7	68·5
Women	42·2	52·4	62·9	74·8

It will be seen from the modified table of the Registrar General statistics[1] that the expectation of life at birth has risen some twenty years for men and twenty-two years for women from the turn of the century. This rise in life expectation brings its timely conclusion near to the biblical notion of three score and ten years. This change is a reflection of the enormous stride made in Western societies in their social and material welfare, particularly through the contribution of medicine. But the change has brought its own mixed blessings, particularly in the case of the elderly, which is one of the challenges facing society.

Of more immediate concern is the differential death rate between the sexes.

TABLE IV

Death Rate per 1000 of Population for 1971

Age	Under 1	1–4	5–44	45–54	55–64	65–74
Men	20	1	1	7	21	52
Women	16	1	1	4	10	27

It will be seen from the table that, with the exception of the second to the forty-fourth year, men are far more vulnerable than women.[2] In particular the death rate rises steeply for men after sixty-five but has a frequency which is double that of women from about the age of fifty-five onwards. This obviously means that mourning is a process which will occur far more frequently in these years in women and there will be far more widows than widowers involved. That most of the recent research on the subject of mourning has involved widows reflects this fact.

The connection between grief, mourning and depression is, in some respects, obvious. Wherever society permits grieving, those who lose their dear ones are acutely distressed, feel and look sad, are liable to weep and have many of the features which are associated with depression. This link was described by Freud in his paper, 'Mourning and melancholia', which began the detailed psychological interest in these two processes of mourning and depression.

For Freud, as for subsequent research workers, the key to the psychology of mourning is the loss of the person (object, in technical terms). This loss is, in the case of death, responsible for the permanent physical departure of another human being, but this physical absence does not eliminate the feelings which belong to the relationship. It is the handling of these feelings which were described in Freud's paper. The medium of explanation was Freud's libido theory, a psychic energy which flowed to and from person to person and within the person himself. This model of psychic energy copied from the physical sciences is no longer in vogue but the observations made on it remain valid.

These observations considered how in mourning there is not only a sense of loss of the departed, but through identification, (i.e., the way we incorporate successfully or otherwise the characteristics of others into ourselves and make them our own) the loss is not only of the other person but of a part, sometimes a substantial one, of ourselves. Secondly, this loss is sometimes interpreted as being the responsibility, the fault, of the mourner, as if he or she actually caused the death. Under these circumstances the loss is treated as the result of damage brought about by the angry feelings towards the deceased which existed prior to death and which were greater than the loving feelings.

The presence concurrently of anger and love is described as ambivalence and it is this ambivalence which may take a severe toll psychologically. If it is marked, the mourner may have to cope with feelings of anger and the possible real or imaginary destructive contribution to the death of the loved one.

One or more of these features may be present in individual instances but these explanations do not give a broad enough interpretation of the psychological process of mourning which has been developing in the last decade.

An authority on this recent work is Dr C. M. Parkes whose book gives detailed descriptions of research of the last ten years.[3] Dr Parkes, working independently at the Maudsley Hospital, reached certain conclusions on grief which had a striking similarity to the thinking of Dr John Bowlby regarding the child's experience of grief when its bond with mother is broken in the course of separation. Dr Parkes joined Dr Bowlby and his research staff at the Tavistock Institute of Human Relations in 1962 and since then, it is no exaggeration to state, some of the most significant developments in dynamic psychology have been emerging from the concepts which were independently initiated by these two doctors. Dr Parkes has concentrated on the field of bereavement but the psychology of human attachment and the consequences of separation, loss and reattachment have widespread universal significance which will go on being examined for some time to come.

The theoretical model proposed by this theory involves consideration of how attachment – and the consequences when it is broken – is established between two living beings, something which has been examined widely in animal species by zoologists (the science of ethology) and described in human beings in the book *Attachment and Loss* by John Bowlby.

The words grief, bereavement, mourning, all apply to human beings and in Chapter V a description was given of the stages through which very young children go between the ages of six months and three years when separated from a key figure in their lives. These phases have been summarized in the terms of protest, despair and detachment. What is described in infancy has universal application, if not in intensity certainly in basic structure, wherever personal bonds are disrupted or, as in the case of death, literally torn apart. Thus the grief experienced by the child in the temporary loss of mother or equivalent important figure is the prototype of a pattern of psychological events whenever something like it occurs and death is a permanent form of loss which could be expected to have similar characteristics. Recent work has shown this to be exactly the case.

The formation and particularly the severance of bonds with which this psychological model is concerned is not something which applies only to human beings; Konrad Lorenz, the father of modern ethology, has written a touching description of this incident in the life of the greylag goose. Here he is describing the loss of its partner.

Even more dramatic . . . is the sudden and shattering loss of the triumph-ceremony partner which must be a frequent happening in the dangerous life of wild geese. The first response to the disappearance of the partner consists in the anxious attempt to find him or her again. The goose moves about restlessly by day and night, flying great distances and visiting all places where the partner might be found, uttering all the time the penetrating trisyllabic long-distance call. This behaviour often calls our attention to the fact that one of our geese is missing. The searching expeditions are extended farther and farther and quite often the searcher itself gets lost or succumbs to an accident. From the moment a goose realizes that the partner is missing it loses all courage and flees even from the youngest and weakest geese. As its condition quickly becomes known to all the numbers of the colony the lonely goose rapidly sinks to the lowest step in the ranking order . . .

All the objectively observable characteristics of the goose's behaviour on losing its mate are roughly identical with those accompanying human grief.[4]

The human grief which concerns us particularly here is the loss of a close relative, particularly a spouse, and the studies of Dr Parkes have shown that the mourning process has similar phases of Alarm, Searching, Protest and Mitigation which resemble the young child's response to loss.

Death is final and irreversible and the human response has to cope with this fact. The child who loses sight of its mother has an expectation of seeing her again, and certainly does not reach the sense of finality with which adults respond to irreversible events.

Even adults find the overwhelming abruptness of death, however much it may have been expected, stunning, and the first reaction to death is a degree of numbness.[5] This is a feeling which comes within a few moments and may last for hours or days; it is described in such terms as – 'Everything goes hard inside' or 'It doesn't seem real.' 'I couldn't take it all in.' 'It doesn't register.'

Following this numbness, reality does begin to register and the reaction is one of fear and alarm, just like that of the child who loses sight and contact with mother. A married couple often have an equally intense closeness and their loss triggers off an alarm reaction, described as a pang of grief and consisting of severe anxiety and psychological pain.

The anxiety response is a common constituent of the depressive picture, particularly when it is triggered off by stress, and usually involves a number of bodily systems. Fear, sometimes increasing to panic, may be present but

usually the feeling is that of 'being on edge', snappy, irritable or easily frightened. Appetite usually suffers and the
whole gastro-intestinal system may become affected with
knotty feelings in the pit of the stomach, nausea, dry mouth,
indigestion pains and loss of weight which at times may
become severe.

The stress is conveyed to the muscles of the body which
respond with tension resulting in headaches located in the
front of the head, and generalized body aches and pains
found anywhere but usually in a site which had given
rise to pain before. Perhaps no other symptom is more
common than loss of, or difficulty in getting off to sleep.
However, the disturbance can continue throughout the
night with fitful, frequently interrupted sleep, sometimes
aggravated by nightmares.

Intimately related to this alarm reaction is that of anger
and irritation which are equivalent to the child's protest.
Anger is expressed by the child through tears, screaming,
shouting, banging, lying on the floor and kicking and generally this frantic activity has a clear goal, namely to bring
mother back. No amount of anger will bring the dead person
back and yet it is generally present in the first year of bereavement in sufficient intensity to be commented upon by
most widows studied in one study.[6]

This anger has several components. The first, and certainly
a most painful one, is the anger arising from the feeling
of being abandoned, the feeling which is so often and aptly
described with the expression – 'Why did you have to do
this to me?' It is understood that few people die (except
in individual suicides) simply to punish those left behind;
nevertheless the pain of abandonment raises angry feelings
based precisely on this sensation.

This anger cannot be easily directed on the dead person
but it can be used against others. Anyone, for example, who
was causing undue worry or making excessive demands on
the deceased. 'They killed him' is an explanation without
much regard to the justice of the complaint. The one source
of possible justification is those who were last in attendance,
namely doctors, nurses, hospital, ambulance drivers. In fact
most relatives are often deeply appreciative of all these

persons but, when the grief is intense, so is the anger and there is a need for scapegoats. There are those, however, who recognize that no one is to blame and, in these circumstances, they may turn their anger inward and blame themselves.

It is not difficult for them to pin blame on themselves. Whatever was done or not done before the death can be used as an excuse. If the husband was asked to do anything, was nagged or criticized, this was the reason, and if he was ignored regarding his clothing, special food fads, his work, his sport, this too could have caused his death. Guilt feelings extend to neglecting early warning signs, and not calling the doctor soon enough, or angry feelings may be entertained because the husband ignored the warning and did not take sufficient advice.

In those instances where there were marital difficulties and persistent angry feelings existed with, for example, a quarrel shortly before the death, guilt feelings can be very marked indeed.

Apart from any unresolved conflicts between spouses, the death of a husband not only generates in the wife a sense of permanent abandonment but also in fact leaves her in a social situation which is full of worry and apprehension. She is concerned, not for her physical survival, but for her personal and social wellbeing. Unless she has been well provided for, a widow is left not only with the acute absence of the most important person in her life but also with the anxiety of picking up the pieces and facing the struggle of material survival. If the husband is young and dies in the prime of life, or in circumstances where her standard of living has to drop – at least temporarily – this can involve having to move house and reducing her standard of living. If there are young children around, their standard of living is also interfered with and sometimes their schooling. Both, of course, if they have to move, lose the support of their friends in their neighbourhood.

Fitting into ordinary life as a single person may present difficulties. A couple is an acceptable and easily integrated unit in social activity but the widow has no clear-cut role and presents problems to her host. None of these are insurmountable but this requires perseverance and the ability to overcome the apprehension that people feel towards the widow whose grief and state is an emotional threat to them. Having said the customary acceptable condolences, how does one comfort further? It is this fear rather than deliberate rejection which makes the plight of widows harsher than it need be. (In fact the isolation and social devaluation of the widow has been recognized by many religions and one answer, admittedly an extremely unsatisfactory one, was the Hindu tradition of Suttee, the wife joining her husband on the funeral pyre.)

This loss of personal standing will decrease as women achieve a social status which reflects their own equal significance, but in the meantime the psychological pain is compounded by social difficulties which, incidentally, were noted in an entirely different setting of the animal kingdom when the 'widowed' goose descends rapidly in the ranking order of its community.

Social readjustment does take place in due course but the immediate psychological reaction, seeking comfort or mitigation, is the equivalent of the child's next phase beyond protest, that of searching. The widow goes through a prolonged phase of searching even though, unlike the child, a part of her knows that this pining is not going to have a successful outcome.

The search may be conscious and deliberate: 'I can't help looking for him everywhere . . . I walk around searching for him.' This intense desire to find the departed person organizes perception in such a way that expectation is high and what is so desperately wanted does come about in a variety of ways.

'Everywhere I go I am searching for him. In crowds, in church, in the supermarket. I keep on scanning the faces. People must think I am odd.'[7] Listening to such an account reminds us of a young child's face as he clings to the side of the cot, his eyes fixed in the direction of the door, attention glued to the slightest signal that heralds the arrival of mother.

And the husband is 'seen'. He is seen in the street, in his car, sitting in his favourite chair, in bed. In a detailed study of 227 Welsh widows and 66 widowers, Rees[8] found that 14 per cent experienced hallucinations or illusions of his or her presence from time to time while 39 per cent had a sense of their presence.

In his study of attachment Bowlby has shown that the means by which this attachment is formed are principally sensory, through touching, seeing, hearing, smelling and it might be expected that these sensations will continue to form the basis of the link between the mourner and the deceased when the latter's presence is strongly evoked. 'I still have the feeling he's near.' 'He's with me all the time. I hear him and see him although I know it's only imagination.' 'I feel he's near me and at times feel his touch.'

Dreams provide a powerful medium of perceptual closeness. The atmosphere of the dream may be comforting or not but the intensity of the contact is very deep. Such dreams can persist for a long time.

> I dream often of my husband. In the dream I am reliving some moment or time together which comes through most vividly. He is really there and I live all over the happenings. I get a lot of joy from these dreams for, although I have come to terms with his death, his presence lives on and I recapture it in the strongest possible way when I dream.

Parkes describes another dream of comfort.

> He was trying to comfort me and putting his arms around me. I kept turning away and crying and crying. Even in the dream I know he's dead . . . But I felt so happy and I cried and he couldn't do anything about it . . . When I touched his face it was as if he was really there – quite real and vivid.

With the passage of time this process of searching and 'finding' recedes and it is sometimes replaced by an encounter with the beloved, which is no longer connected with the immediate need to have physical sensations, but rather with a feeling of meeting the whole deceased person which can become an enduring sense of closeness. C. S. Lewis describes such an encounter in his diary.

Something quite unexpected has happened. It came this morning early. For various reasons, not in themselves at all mysterious, my heart was lighter than it had been for many weeks. For one thing, I suppose I am recovering physically . . . the sun was shining and there was a light breeze. And suddenly at the very moment when, so far, I mourned H. least, I remembered her best. Indeed, it was something (almost) better than memory; an instantaneous, unanswerable impression. To say it was like a meeting would go too far. Yet there was that in it which tempts me to use those words. It was as if the lifting of the sorrow removed a barrier.

The last phase of separation for the young child is total loss of the attachment to the parent when the memory is lost for good and, if she returns, a new form of attachment has to be formed, almost reattachment. After death detachment does in fact take place, and slowly, over a period of a year, the period of severe grief is over. But adult relationships which have lasted many years leave their imprint and become part of the survivor and the memory of the dead remains a reality which survives the sorrow of the mourning process.

The process of grieving or mourning just described has a depressive quality permeating throughout its component elements. And yet the process is undoubtedly a normal one, just as the grieving experience of the child is a normal response to the loss of a mother or mother substitute. In both instances, what is seen is the appropriate human response to bond splitting and, with our present knowledge, we are describing what seems to be a fundamental human psychological mechanism which has the characteristics of a depressive reaction.

Mourning and its grief illustrate some of the difficulties encountered in the description of depression and its management. At what point do we have distress that is abnormal following an illness model and when do we have a normal and inescapable human reaction which should not be con-

D   E

sidered as an illness?

This point, which will strike the reader in many parts of the book, is truly one of the perplexing and confusing aspects of describing and handling depression to which we shall return again in the chapter on treatment.

As far as mourning is concerned, one way of defining the beginnings of an illness process is by describing the atypical. If enough studies are made of the average response of widowhood, then we have a criterion of what to expect as part of the normal course or the natural history of mourning. This is where Dr Parkes's studies have given so much original information and it is by comparing the course of a particular person with that taken by the average that the atypical, and therefore the pathological or the group that needs extra support, can begin to emerge.

Perhaps the first point to be made here is that it is abnormal, atypical *not* to mourn someone close and beloved. In a society which has placed its trust on material progress, concentrated its attention on the here and now, has lost the familiarity of early death through the enormous strides of medicine, a certain avoidance of the painful confrontation with death and mourning can be expected. Gorer, who made a study of the subject[9] has commented that 'Mourning is treated as if it were a weakness, a self indugence, a reprehensible bad habit of a psychological necessity.'

The person who refuses or cannot mourn is behaving abnormally and this abnormality shows itself in at least two other ways. The process can be delayed, unduly prolonged or intensified to the point that medical intervention is needed.

Those who cannot accept the death live for a while with the well-known psychological mechanism of denial. Although something clearly has happened, the person psychologically lives as if it had not. The initial shock is prolonged and the person goes on as if they had not lost their spouse who they insist is around. One such woman had to be admitted to hospital where she continued to insist that her husband was alive. At home she sat by the window hour after hour and, when darkness came, put on the outside light. She refused to eat until he joined her at table or go to bed without his presence. In conversation she vehemently denied his death. Soon exhaustion took over and she was admitted to hospital. It took a number of weeks before she could accept the fact and then begin the process of mourning with weeping, grief and marked depression.

The time taken to mourn varies from person to person but most of the severe manifestations are receding by the end of the first year and so marked persistence beyond twelve months would indicate an atypical or abnormal reaction.

In addition to prolongation, the intensity of the response is also an indication of severity. One widow had to be hospitalized for this reason. Her reaction was intense for the first few months of her loss. Severe weeping, loss of sleep, appetite and weight continued months afterwards. She spent a great deal of her time at the cemetery, in all types of weather, ignoring her own physical condition and unable to look after her children.

The clearest indication of the pathological, the abnormal, is the supervening of a depressive illness in which the depression has the characteristics of involving extensively all the physical and mental systems in a typical depressive way. Dr Parkes studied this by comparing the diagnoses of 94 patients who had been admitted within six months of the death of a parent, spouse, brother, sister or child with 3151 non-bereaved admissions. There was a clear-cut higher incidence of affective disorders and, particularly, the diagnosis of reactive depression.

A delayed, prolonged or intense mourning may in fact distinguish between normal and abnormal or pathological mourning. In these circumstances the safety of the patient, both in protecting his good health and guarding against the risk of suicide, may require admission to hospital or at least active treatment for the depressive state.

Are there any distinctive characteristics which make the bereaved particularly vulnerable? Dr Parkes provides an excellent account which summarizes the main points.

From the evidence available, which comes mostly from the study of bereaved women rather than bereaved men, our high-risk case would be a young widow with chil-

dren living at home and no close relatives living by. She
would be a timid, clinging person who had reacted badly
to separation in the past and had a previous history of
depressive illness. Closely bound up with her husband
in an over-reliant or ambivalent relationship, she would
not have prepared herself for his unexpected and untimely
death. Cultural and familial tradition would prevent her
from expressing the feelings that then threatened to
emerge.

Other stresses occurring before or after his bereavement
– such as loss of income, change of home and difficulties
with children – would increase her burden. Although she
may at first appear to be coping well, intense pining would
subsequently emerge, together with evidence of pronounced self-reproach and/or anger.

Having said this we must remind ourselves that we
are speaking only in terms of probabilities. A person may
fit all these predictions and still not break down after
bereavement, or they may have none of them and yet
break down. In an infinitely variable world, there is
infinite room for variation.[10]

The admission to a mental hospital or psychiatric unit
is an indication that the mourning process has reached depressive illness proportions which require treatment.

Is there any evidence to support the view that, although
mourning is a normal event which needs to be experienced
to some degree by everyone, in certain instances it has a
markedly adverse effect on health which requires medical
attention?

This evidence does exist and takes different forms. In a
classification of the causes of death in 1657 the following are
listed:

Flox and Small Pox	835
Found dead in the street, etc.	9
French Pox	25
Gout	8
Griefe	10
Gripping and Plague in the Guts	446
Hang'd and made away 'emselves	24

Dr Heberden's Bill has considerable sociological interest to our modern eyes. Nowadays infectious disease takes a very small toll of life provided the appropriate vaccination and immunization programmes are undertaken so that one of the principal causes of death has been removed. Equally we would be shocked to find anybody dead in the street from neglect, malnutrition or disease although this still occurs in other parts of the world. We no longer hang our criminals but suicide remains a cause of death.

What is particularly striking in this list is the category of 'Griefe'. Certainly poets and prose writers have described the distress of loss and this has commonly been interpreted as poetic, artistic licence but, until recently, this item on the list would have been dismissed with incredulity and scorn. Now we would not be so sure.

An extensive study centred on the small market town of Llanidloes, covering a semi-rural area of a population of 5184, was carried out over a period of six years. During these six years 488 residents died. 371 of these people had close relatives living in the survey area and the subsequent mortality of their 913 close relatives was compared with that of a control group. The control group was composed of the 878 close relatives of 371 people matched by age, sex and marital state with the people who originally died.[11]

It was found that 4.76 per cent of bereaved close relatives died within one year of the bereavement compared with 0.68 per cent in the control group. This is a sevenfold increase and is statistically highly significant, that is to say, the likelihood of it occurring through random chance was very low indeed. Furthermore, the risk was greater for male than female relatives, the risk being 6.4 per cent and 3.5 per cent.

Figure 1 shows these features clearly, and also another point. For example, 11.6 per cent of the survey group died within a year of bereavement and the corresponding figure for the control group was 1.6 per cent, a figure which remains pretty constant over a five year period. The raised mortality rate for the relatives of the deceased people remains high, although not so high, for some three years and does not reach the same incidence as the control until the fourth year.

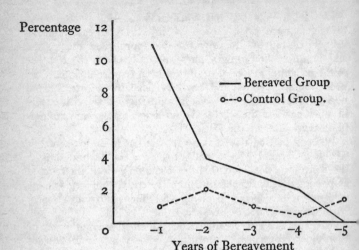

Figure 1. Percentage of deceased people whose
death was followed each year by the death
of a close relative.

Of the close relatives who had a higher incidence of
death, the widowed spouse headed the list and in the first
year 12.2 per cent died compared with 1.2 per cent of the
control group. Furthermore, widowers died far more frequently than widows, 19.6 per cent compared with 8.5 per
cent and the peak period of mortality was during the first
6 months, also confirmed in another study.[12] Additional data
pertaining to all males over the age of 54 in England and
Wales whose wives died during two months of 1957 showed
that in the first 6 months of bereavement the mortality rate
was 40 per cent higher than the expected rate based on
national figures for married men of the same age.[13]

A detailed examination of the death certificates of these
deaths showed that 75 per cent of the increased death rate
during the first six months was accounted for by diseases
of the heart, particularly coronary thrombosis and arterio-
sclerotic heart disease. Benjamin Rush, an American physician
and signatory of the Declaration of Independence, wrote

in 1835, 'Dissection of persons who have died of grief, showed congestion and inflammation of the heart, with rupture of its auricles and ventricles.'

The condition described by Benjamin Rush is in fact extremely rare but the poetic notion of the broken heart seems to have found support even though the connecting link is not precise. The link will be undoubtedly found in the relationship between the psychological stress of bereavement and the associated physical impact on the body.

Increased mortality of close relatives, particularly the spouse, is the ultimate indication of the psycho-physical turbulence of mourning. There is also further evidence which, as would be expected, involves deterioration of health. Such deterioration can be measured by the subjective report of the widowed or the objective information derived from their family doctors and from questionnaires. Evidence is available from all these sources to show the adverse effects.

Thus, in a study[14] of 72 unselected widows interviewed in London, on an average two years after bereavement, 43 per cent thought their health had deteriorated. In another study in the Midlands,[15] the figure was 42 per cent and in yet another 27 per cent. No one claimed that their health had improved subsequent to the death of their spouse.[16]

These descriptions do not necessarily mean that the person has to attend his doctor; but in fact a detailed study of eight London general practices was able to show that the consultation rate went up markedly after a bereavement compared to a two year period before. There was a sharp rise from 2.2 consultations per patient per six month period before the bereavement which increased to 3.6 consultations during the first six months after the bereavement.[17]

An analysis of the specific symptoms[18] that are complained of in this situation has been made in another study and the following show a high frequency – headache, indigestion, vomiting, poor or excessive appetite, weight loss, palpitations, chest pain, dyspepsia, frequent infection and general aching.

All these symptoms are consistent with the alarm or anxiety state, found in the bereavement reaction and only two require comment. The first is excessive appetite which at first sight was contradictory and out of place with the rest. Appetite is an instinctual drive which is linked with a controlling centre in the hypothalamus in the brain. Stress appears to be capable of initiating either a reduction or an excess of appetite and some people find themselves compelled to eat excessive amounts at times of crisis and stress, thus putting on large amounts of weight. The second point is the presence of frequent infection.[19] It is known that debilitated people, for a variety of reasons, tend to succumb far more frequently to colds, infections of the bladder, boils, chest infections and what appears to be a general lowering of bodily resistance.

The most likely reasons for attending the doctor, however, are the more specific feelings of 'being on edge', feeling irritable, tending to snap at people, weeping, depression and insomnia. These psychological symptoms are, of course, very much in line with the symptoms of a depressive illness and ultimately it is the diagnosis of depression which could necessitate admission to hospital.

As already indicated, symptoms of bereavement abate gradually by the end of the first year only to have a sudden reappearance round about the period of the anniversary. The anniversary period is the time of sharp reminder when the deceased assumes once again a vivid meaning which can become powerful enough to trigger off the same manifestations in a slight, moderate or severe form. Usually the time passes with a minimum of distress symptoms or feelings but occasionally a severe grief reaction or even depression can be stirred up by the occasion.

The anniversary, however, becomes the last hazard of bereavement, one of the most universal of human experiences which spares no one and which fits in with Samuel Butler's aphorism that it is death and not what comes after death that men are generally afraid of.

Notes

1. H.M.S.O., (1969), *Registrar-General Review*, London, Table B.2, p. 11
2. H.M.S.O., (1972), *Social Trends*, No. 3, London; Table 3, p. 60.
3. Parkes, C. M., (1972), *Bereavement*, Tavistock Publications, London
4. Lorenz, K., (1967), *On Aggression*, Methuen University Paperback, London, pp. 78-9
5. Parkes, *op. cit.*, p. 65
6. Parkes, C. M., (1971), 'The First Year of Bereavement', *Psychiatry*: 33:444
7. Parkes, *Bereavement*, p. 47
8. Rees, W. D., (1970), *The Hallucinating and Paranormal Reactions of Bereavement*, M.D. Thesis
9. Gorer, G., (1965), *Grief and Mourning in Contemporary Britain*, London
10. Parkes, *Bereavement*, p. 147
11. Rees, W. D., Lutkins, S. G., (1967), 'Mortality of Bereavement', *British Medical Journal*, 4:13
12. Young, M., Benjamin, B., Wallis, (1963), *Lancet* 2; 454
13. Parkes, C. M., Benjamin, B., Fitzgerald, R. G., (1969), 'Broken Heart: A statistical study of increased mortality among widowers', *British Medical Journal*, 1, 740
14. Marris, P., (1958), *Widows and their Families*, Routledge and Kegan Paul, London
15. Hobson, C. J., (1964), 'Widows of Blackton', *New Society* 24, Sept. 13
16. Parkes, C. M., (1970), 'The Psychomatic Effects of Bereavement' in *Psychomatic Medicine* 2, Ed. Oscar Hill, Butterworth, London
17. Parkes, C. M., (1964), 'Effects of Bereavement on Physical and Mental Health: A study of the Medical Records of Widows', *British Medical Journal* 2, 274
18. Madison, I. C., Walker, W. L., (1967), *British Journal of Psychiatry*, 113, 1057
19. Madison, I. C., Viola, A., (1968), *Journal of Psychosomatic Research*, 12:297

XII Dying and Depression

The previous chapter described our response to personal loss. Much of the description was taken up with the death of the spouse, although many of the features of bereavement apply to all losses of relatives or friends with whom there exists a close bond. The characteristic of bereavement is grief and many of the features of grief are those which describe a mood swing of a depressive type.

Depression is also a prominent feature in the terminal period of those who are dying slowly from a physical condition which has gone beyond cure. Many of these conditions are untreatable cancers but by no means all of them; for example, serious damage to lungs, kidneys, liver tissue or severe heart failure are all conditions which herald death, with the patient frequently longing for this to be the case.

Observations in recent years have shown that, while the inevitability of death carries its own unavoidable distress, which again can be understood to be a separation anxiety, this time not for one person but for everything which is meaningful, nevertheless depression may supervene and add a gloom and distress of its own which is not an essential part of dying.

In a study of psychological reactions in those dying in hospital, Professor J. Hinton found that within two weeks before death no less than half of the patients were experiencing some depression of mood.[1] Such a mood, which shows itself by withdrawal, loss of interest and the capacity to enjoy or be in touch with daily events, is normally accounted for by the seriousness of the illness. This is a wrong assumption in that others who are seriously ill but have hopes of recovery do not experience the same degree of suffering.[2]

This noticeable degree of depression associated with serious physical illness takes its toll not only in the suffering of depression but in anticipating death through suicide. In a study of suicides in an East Anglian urban area, an examination of the records of thirty suicides covering a seven year period showed that no less than 14 were suffering from physical illness which was markedly higher than in a control group.[3] Other studies[4] confirm this and sometimes a further tragedy emerges in some of those who killed themselves because of the fear of cancer when the postmortem showed that treatment had controlled the disease and there was no evidence of recurrence.

What contributes to this depression? Patients tend to get progressively more depressed as the illness lengthens and particularly if physical pain and distress persist unrelieved. There is good evidence indicating that the successful control of pain is a potent source of relief not only for the physical distress but also for the mental state.

The adequate relief of physical pain is a point made by Dr Cecily Saunders, a pioneer worker in this country in the care of the dying, but she also makes the far more important point which is that the attitude to the dying is of equal importance.[5] She emphasizes the importance of listening, which of course requires the overcoming of the fears that lie between the dying and those near them. A great deal of controversy surrounds the topic of whether people should be told or not about their approaching death but Cecily Saunders reverses the process and says, in an address to doctors, which however could apply equally to all those close to the dying:

The real question is not, – 'What do you tell your patients?' but rather – 'What do you let your patients tell you?'[6]

If the depressed dying patient was given the opportunity to ventilate his feelings, what would in fact preoccupy him? Each person has his own unique life style with its special meaning but some features are present in common.

Perhaps the first point is the mixture of feelings regarding the need to have company and friendship and the fear that his appearance will distress his visitors. If the visitor shows clear signs of fear and looks uncomfortable, then this will be registered by the dying person who recognizes that it is his condition which is provoking it. Nevertheless the need for closeness and communication can be strong.

In the course of bereavement angry feelings of being abandoned may be experienced. The possibility has to be considered that the dying feel they are being abandoned by relatives and friends. Irritation and anger can be experienced by them, particularly if they are young and feel that life is being grossly unfair, cheating them of their just dues. Such an attitude may enhance depression, particularly if these feelings cannot be expressed.

Another feature of the anger is the frustration of helplessness, as their own capacity to look after themselves and control their own destiny wanes. Such physical deterioration may be due to pain, weakness or severe deterioration of breathing. The person fighting for his breath is an acutely distressed person and may experience marked anger that he should be denied a faculty that everybody else takes for granted without having to struggle for it.

This inability to look after themselves and to function effectively becomes a powerful threat to their meaning as a person. If someone has relied exclusively for their personal significance on their ability to do things, to communicate through action, to find their gratification by what they have accomplished, then the loss of such an activity virtually deprives them of their single most important way of being human.

Fears crowd in that they are about to be thrown into the dustbin, on to the human scrap heap of the obsolete and redundant, without any further use. As they see the family and their work colleagues survive and function well, they are seized with an even greater fear, namely that they are better out of the way and that everybody will cope much better without them.

Provided those surrounding the dying person can actually open themselves to receive these distressed feelings, then a great deal of the depressive mood can lift. The reason for their embarrassment is the feeling that nothing can be done. Much, of course, can be done to relieve pain and distress but, even more important, much can be done by listening, not for the purpose of changing the course of the disease, but making it possible for the patient to realize fully his or her potential until death. Dr Cicely Saunders summarizes this point: 'The aim of such communication and of such treatment is that the patient should both be relieved of his distress and remain himself, helped not only to die peacefully but also to *live* until he dies.'[7]

The responsibility of listening is one to be shared by doctors, nurses, relatives and friends but it is the relatives who will subsequently undergo the bereavement and it would appear that a double burden of distress may be imposed upon them, both by listening and remaining open to the inner fears of the dying and by grieving afterwards. In fact the process of grieving can benefit enormously by the sharing which has taken place beforehand and which allows the fullest communication to take place.

Dying is not only a meeting point between being and non-being; it also highlights attitudes to religion and any belief in the hereafter.

In a recent book[8] which has surveyed world-wide attitudes and has shown that, although belief in God (with all the ambiguity that the word implies) remains high in Europe – in fact of the order between 60 per cent and 96 per cent – belief in life after death is almost half, ranging from 35 per cent to 57 per cent.

This decline is part of the consistent picture of the gap between belief in God and religious practice in the traditional forms of all denominations. Having a formal faith may be no more than a gesture to custom and habit with no penetrating implication for the individual. It is the impact of faith on the whole personality which gives meaning and ultimate purpose and which acts as a source of sustenance and strength at the time of death. But Christianity in its various forms has been going through intense and agonizing self-criticism. A moving personal account of the life of one woman captures vividly many of the psychological points described above in a religious setting and also shows some of the reasons which have alienated millions from the Christian faith which used to provide one powerful source of consolation at death.

In my case, it was towards the age of two that I first became acquainted with death. A serious pulmonary infection brought on an apnoea (cessation of breathing), simulating actual death . . .

From my earliest childhood I lived a marginal existence in relation to my brothers and sisters. They could do whatever they pleased: they were in good health . . .

When I was just five (and not yet attending school), I was accidentally scalded. Only my face was spared. I was reduced to a raw wound, howling with pain . . .

Sedatives calmed me for a time and then I began again to scream with pain. All attempts to soothe me proved useless. Then the doctor told me what I now call, with some bitterness, 'my first fairy-tale'. As I recall (and this is confirmed by my mother who was present), he told me that beyond the clouds there is a wonderful place called Heaven, which is the home of Jesus. If I stopped crying and moaning 'Little Jesus' would come and fetch me to play with him in that wonderful castle full of toys, speaking dolls and even animals (I loved cats). When I objected that I did not want to be separated from my mummy, he replied that she would not go with me straight away but would join me very shortly. 'In heaven,' he added, 'little children are never sick and have no wounds. Little Jesus has the power to heal everything' . . .

After a few weeks I was untied from my bed so that I could sit in an armchair, yet I still had to undergo very painful treatment to prevent scarring. I understood that I would not die, in other words that Jesus would not come and fetch me, probably because I had not been good enough. I also thought sadly of the dreadful sinners whom I had not saved because I had cried.

On looking back I feel that I emerged from this period of my life with my soul more scarred than my body. The doctor's words, having probably aggravated a pre-existing guilt complex, had caused me to form false ideas of God, heaven, death and life. God, that Child Jesus, made demands that were impossible to fulfil in return for a friendship whose proof – or so I believed – lay in his readiness to come and fetch me, in other words by making me die. When I got better I was looked upon as a 'miraculous healed person' whereas I was more inclined to think of myself as a girl 'who had not been considered worthy'. From that time onwards, I regarded life as a punishment and death as a reward that I had failed to merit despite my efforts . . .

Between the ages of five and fifteen, to all outward appearances, uneventful apart from a few additions to my case history — a tonsillectomy with post-operative haemorrhages, diphtheria — my parents continued to worry about me but I was undisturbed. Since I always managed to escape death, the thought of it ceased to haunt me.

Towards the age of fifteen, life reasserted itself. I became lively and flirtatious, and fell in love with a boy-friend as one does at that age. Since my health had improved, my parents sent me to a boarding school to make up for the gaps in my education, which had been inevitably neglected because of my frequent absences from school. After six months at boarding school, I developed an unforeseen and malignant tuberculosis.

Once again I found myself at death's door and it was generally felt that I had no hope of getting better. My parents and the doctor decided not to warn me of the nature and gravity of the illness. But an austere and neurotic priest, who was an old college friend of my father, thought it advisable that I should know I was 'fatally ill'. He considered that no one had the right to cheat me of my death . . .

This is how he broke the news to me: 'I have to tell you now that you've developed tuberculosis. The doctor holds out no hope of curing you . . . or very little. The disease may run its course very quickly, but he says that with good care your life may be kept going for another six months. Humanly speaking, it distresses me, but from the spiritual point of view I'm glad, for at this moment I'm certain that you'll go to heaven, whereas in six months from now, can I be so sure?'

This time I positively rebelled: 'I don't want to die and I won't die! Why should it happen to me and not others?'

'You have nothing to gain by resisting God's will. The date of your death is recorded in the "Great Book" and however much you rebel, you can't do anything about it.'

I then made some remarks that were blasphemous in their intention if not in their actual words. I was blazing with the bitter hatred of my rebellion against God. This time I would not let myself be bribed with toys or the promise of Jesus's companionship. I wanted life and I would allow no one to rob me of it . . .

When I saw the priest again, I told him once more of my despair, my desire to live, to be loved, to have children of my own. 'There you are', he replied. 'You haven't any yet and perhaps that's the very reason why the good Lord is taking you in the place of a father whose death would leave his children in want' . . .

I immediately thought of my father and of the seven orphans whom his death would bereave. I would offer my life for his: that would make my death meaningful. I therefore resigned myself to the thought of dying, but on one condition: that I should die quickly and without waiting for weeks on end. True death is not the one that occurs when the heart stops beating: it is the death that overtakes you gradually so that you cannot even tell whether you will still be alive on the following Sunday . . .

After a year, I was no longer infectious but my condition remained stationary. My parents asked to take me home. And there, after a few weeks, a miracle occurred. Every night, without telling my parents, I fetched books from our library and read them. Then a veil was torn asunder, shaking my inward life to the core. I owe that miracle to two books: *The Confessions* of St Augustine and *The Words of a Ghost* by Jacques Arnoux. The first revealed to me a God of Love who is never out of patience with our weaknesses, our failures, our lapses and our cries. The second taught me that, in order to be healed, one has to will it and strive for it every hour of the day. I was suddenly freed from the world of death in which I had lived since my birth. Externally, nothing had changed. But within me everything had been transformed: I had the right to desire to live, to ask for health, to strive for it. I began to take an interest in others and not merely in my small person and its preoccupation with death.

In the Bible, which I began to read daily, I discovered a God whom I had not known hitherto. Reading the Book of Job comforted me. He had rebelled before submitting himself to the divine will. I learnt to pray, to ask for healing by telling the Lord that I would make something of my life, that I would devote myself to the care of the sick.

At the age of twenty I decided to train as a nurse. The doctors and my parents were against it, then consented, telling themselves that I might persevere for a month and would soon be rid of my fancies. Physically, the first months were very hard, but I was so happy to be of use to others. When I went off duty, I would go into the hospital chapel and say to the Lord – 'You, who healed the paralysed and the blind, accept my weariness so that I may have the strength to start again tomorrow morning.' They were extraordinary months and to me they seemed to be the very first months of my life.

Half a year later, my father – who was only forty-eight – had a serious illness. He died within a year. According to my mother, his health had begun to deteriorate when I left home. I felt guilty. Could it be that the Lord had come to fetch him because I had no longer been willing to die?

My healthier relationship with God enabled me to overcome this feeling of guilt (but not without difficulty).

Since those early days, years have gone by. I still think of death every single day, but so that I may love life even more.

This autobiographical statement is included, not only as a remarkable personal document of human courage and perseverance, but also because within it will be found illustrated many aspects of the complex feelings, including the depressive ones of those facing death as well as the progress of medicine, particularly in the care of tuberculosis, where the whole of the death scene and its world of depressive despair has virtually disappeared with modern forms of treatment.

The writer blames no one, but millions have found this form of Christianity unacceptable and irrelevant and have not made the breakthrough she did. This is a breakthrough into the meaning of life as something to be fully lived, minute by minute, instead of submerging it into a living grave as a preparation for a future life. She found faith in the hope and life of the here and now and invites others to tackle life, however limited, in the same vein. Certainly such faith which involves the whole person through and through has an impact on the way that death is approached.

Hinton found that in those with a deep sense of faith only a fifth were apprehensive about their approaching death. The next most confident group, in which only a quarter were anxious, were those who had frankly said they had practically no faith. The tepid believers, who professed faith but made little outward observance of it, were far more anxious. They were twice as commonly apprehensive as either the regular churchgoers or those without religious faith.[10]

What these findings clearly indicate is that the most likely basis of dispelling the gloom of approaching death is the presence of a personality whose inner foundation has clear, strong and reliable meaning. The person needs to feel that life makes sense even though it is about to dissolve.

Christians feel that the framework of reference which gives them coherence is their faith, provided it is held in a way that does not violate human integrity. But this is certainly not the only possible answer. There are other forms of religion which can give such an integrated meaning provided they are followed faithfully, and unbelievers can also have a system of belief which, without admitting God, makes a systematic sense of life. Here is such a person describing his attitude to death.

In reality we die a little every day. That hive of cells, which we are at a given moment, gradually breaks up its connecting links and disrupts its own harmony. Although the surrendering is a fact and unpleasant, of course, to envisage, it enables man to be in greater possession of himself and gently obliges him, if you think about it, to acknowledge his own limitation . . . As a biologist, I'm aware that life has been given to us with all the hazards of heredity which has made us what we are. And yet, if our life has been fashioned for us, if – in the first place – one has sufficiently respected the personality of others, if in addition one has left in the heart of a few fellow men a feeling of affection and friendship, then there's no such thing as real death.[11]

There will always be arguments about the truth of any particular system of belief, hence the debate between believers and non-believers but, as far as the dying person is concerned, what really matters is that the threat of physical extinction can be related to an emotional acceptance so that relationships with others – and therefore with oneself – will preserve the best aspect of life and give it purposeful meaning until the very end.

Notes

1. Hinton, J., (1967), *Dying*, Pelican Books, Harmondsworth, p. 85
2. *Ibid.*, p. 84
3. Jones, K., (1965), 'Suicide and the Hospital Service', *British Journal of Psychiatry*, 111, 625
4. Sainsbury, P., (1955), *Suicide in London*, Chapman & Hall, London
5. Saunders, C., (1970), *The Nature and Management of Terminal Pain* in *Matters of Life and Death*, Darton, Longman & Todd, London
6. *Ibid.*, p. 16
7. *Ibid.*, pp. 16-17
8. Godin, A., Ed., (1972), *Death and Presence. The Psychology of Death and After Life*, Lumen Vitae, Brussels
9. *Ibid.*, pp. 74ff
10. Hinton, *op. cit.*, p. 83
11. Godin, *op. cit.*, p. 44

XIII   The Management of Depression

In this and the next two chapters we will look at the question of the management and treatment of depression. The reader may legitimately ask at this stage – 'Yes, we now know something of the various ways that depression shows itself but what should be done about it, when should help be sought and from whom?'

All these are legitimate questions to which there are no perfect or precise answers. If a person has a pain in their stomach, a doctor is called in who makes the appropriate diagnosis, be it appendicitis, perforated ulcer, gall bladder colic, intestinal spasm or one of the other possibilities. In all these situations there is usually a commonly agreed medical answer. In some cases it is an emergency operation, in others more conservative medical treatment.

But in all instances the presence of severe pain, disturbed function, possibly fever and generalized disturbances makes it imperative that action be taken. When this model of diagnosis and treatment to which we are all accustomed is transferred to psychiatry, several snags are encountered.

In psychiatry there are rarely physical symptoms or objective laboratory investigations to confirm the subjective distress of patients. Everything depends on what they feel, how they act and how others see and assess them. In this world of subjective feelings, mood and its variations is a continuous process. Persistent pain is invariably a warning of disturbed function, whereas changes of mood are part and parcel of everyday life.

Thus the first difficulty which exists in answering the question of treatment is that of disentangling the difference between normal and abnormal depressive reactions. The former can be considered as an acceptable element of daily living, the latter as a variation which is no longer of benefit and, indeed, may be harmful to the wellbeing of the individual and needs treatment. Many problems lie precisely in defining the point of transition from one to the other. There are no absolute indicators but there are some useful pointers.

The change in mood towards depression joins two other human features, pain and anxiety, and between them these three characteristics – physical pain, psychological anxiety and depression – constitute a triad which acts as a signalling system of distress. The unpleasant quality which is always present acts as a warning, a kind of human radar which scans the reality of life and gives our appropriate response. In the case of pain and anxiety, personal survival may be at stake; in the case of mood, this may also be true but, as a rule, it acts as a guide to the meaning and significance of personal events. To eliminate or render unnecessary any one of the three is to deprive life of one of its essentials.

If this particular interpretation is accepted, then clearly it has a bearing on the philosophy and expectation of a society. The philosophy concerns the meaning of suffering and the expectation the point at which it should be abolished. The advent of powerful and wide-ranging medication which can remove symptoms has also brought with it important ethical questions of how this medication should be used. If the intervention is too early and too hasty, it is likely that a person is being deprived of a necessary experience in his or her life; if there is neglect and the intervention is too late, depression can cost a life. In between there lies a whole range of suffering which has as much potential for good as it does for being destructive and wasteful. Ultimately this is a personal decision, the fruit of which may not be seen for several years afterwards. It is a decision which increasingly preoccupies our society which is part of a civilization in which religion in its various forms, but particularly the Judeao-Christian tradition, laid down the ideology and the moral principles governing suffering.

People simply accepted these moral principles without too much questioning. Now there is relentless questioning of religion and morality with a wide range of independent and uncoordinated answers. This may be a temporary phase until new values emerge which can give rise to a consensus of standards. In the interval the amount of suffering is a private decision and a good deal of it arises from a depressive reaction to life events. When is it justifiable and at what point should steps be taken to alleviate it?

In general terms two features of the depressive process can act as a guide here. First, is the depression part of a necessary process? By a necessary process we mean negotiating a happening which is inevitable or necessary for maturation. The second is the question of emotional growth.

Under the category of inevitable are to be found all irretrievable losses. A loss may involve a person, a thing, a social situation or a part of oneself. Departure and death of a loved one at all stages of life bring about an irretrievable loss, the former being temporary and the latter permanent. Losses of objects depend on their personal value. Anything can bring a depressive reaction but common objects are money, valuables (of high or low value), gifts from significant people, anything with special meaning or which has taken a great deal of effort to attain and irreplaceable items. Losses of a social nature mean a loss in standing, prestige, influence, power and appreciation. Finally, personal loss may be physical in losing a vital organ or psychological in the loss of the love and care, or approval, of somebody significant in our lives.

In all these instances sadness is a proper and inevitable reaction which acts as a stimulus to make up for the loss. This compensation is an adaptative process which can take place by replacement or learning how to cope effectively without the presence of the lost object (person or thing). Sadness or depression acts as a stimulus towards the healing of the wound, as a means of perseverance until a new situation of adjustment has been reached. The lives of individuals who have overcome marked physical defects such as blindness, deafness, paralysis or a combination of all three, are part of the rich heritage of society and almost invariably all of them include overcoming a depressive element. The anonymous nurse quoted in the previous chapter, as well as thousands of others, could fill this book with innumerable examples in which a deep personal misery inflicts on the sufferer a state of depression, sometimes approaching despair, which becomes a challenge first to survive and second to be conquered. Nor is this a recent discovery by man. Job's lament is a reminder of a depressive outcry which has its echoes recurring throughout history, a cry directed at God or man. Job is venting his feelings of despair at God.

> If only my misery could be weighed,
> And all my ills be put on scales!
> But they outweigh the sands of the seas;
> What wonder then if my words are wild? 6: 2-3

> And now the life in me trickles away,
> Days of grief have gripped me.
> At night time, sickness saps my bones,
> I am gnawed by wounds that never sleep. 30: 16-17

The response to such depressive feelings is either resignation or fight, and in either case the hasty removal of the depressive mood would be wholly inappropriate, just as — even if we had the means of removing hunger (modified attempts do exist) or thirst — we would not consider it normal to eliminate either, since the removal of the distress could ultimately kill the person.

Accepting that a depressive reaction is a necessary process in the response to loss, the second feature we must look at is emotional growth. Physical growth is visible and measurable; intellectual growth is not so easily detectable or measurable but psychological tests and examinations give crude measures. What is more difficult to see, measure or define is emotional growth.

Emotional growth involves several factors. Primarily it covers the world of feelings. The capacity to feel, accurately judge one's own feelings and those of others and handle them in such a manner that love is greater than anger and destruction towards oneself or others, becomes the ultimate goal of emotional growth. This ultimate goal requires patience and increasing effort so that gradually self-acceptance, self-esteem reaches a point where we can sufficiently accept our own goodness without being helplessly dependent on others. Having achieved this, we can recognize and accept responsibility for our damaging actions, seek forgiveness, and accept it from others having made the necessary reparation.

All this takes time and needs to negotiate critical periods in life, such as adolescence and middle age. Both adolescence and middle age can bring a crop of depressive reactions which have been described in Chapters VII and X respectively. Removing the depressed mood in any of these circumstances is potentially unhelpful to the necessary growth that has to take place.

Does this mean that the presence of what has here been described as an inevitable process is an absolute contra-indication to seeking or receiving help? Whatever answer may be given in these pages, it would be irrelevant because in fact human beings do seek this help from each other. They seek it from relatives, friends, pastors, anonymously from journals, advice centres; in fact from a whole variety of sources. People will always turn to these sources for help. But suppose these resources are not sufficient; what is the answer? Do we tell such people simply to pull themselves together? Do we adopt an attitude of condescending superiority?

People would be horrified if they were told they were callous or rejecting, but unwittingly they may appear to be so by applying the following 'common-sense' approach. 'We had the same problems, we got depressed, we persevered, we pulled ourselves together, why don't you? The answer is you don't want to. You are not trying hard enough. You are lazy. You are this. You are that. Go away and try harder.'

One such person, having received such advice, has put her feelings down in the following brief statement.

How can anyone who has never experienced the condition of depression, have any conception of the darkness of mind, emotion and soul, that engulfs one? It is no consolation to be told that everyone has problems — particularly when one is not aware of any problems which would produce a state of depression. The prevailing emotion is one of being an encumbrance to others, of being incapable of making any worthwhile contribution to society. Slowly and painfully you try to pick yourself up and make a fresh start, only to have one's face, metaphorically speaking, rubbed in the mud of previous failures. Presumably, all those who read out a little lesson, kindly or not, or tell you to 'pull yourself together' intend this to help you. But it simply makes one even more painfully aware of one's deficiencies.

One result of psychological research is the increasing awareness that there are certain individuals who need help if they are to negotiate their loss or critical moments in life.

By help we mean here help additional to that to which they already have recourse. As a group, such men and women have certain common characteristics. They find it very difficult to mix with others and so at all times – but particularly in adolescence – they are unable to make the necessary contact, to socialize, which gives individual or group reassurance. Their isolation, arising out of shyness and inability to make easy contact – particularly with the opposite sex – reinforces or initiates a sense of personal inadequacy which makes contact even more difficult. This establishes a vicious circle which is hard to break and within which the person gets increasingly depressed and dispirited.

This isolation, coupled with a sense of inadequacy, makes them liable to feel that others can see their shortcomings miles away, are likely to be critical, laugh at them and ridicule them and so they keep their distance. When they receive praise or appreciation, they find it difficult to believe it is truly meant for them and they become suspicious that it is not sincerely meant for them or that it is a prelude to some exploitation.

Here a girl expresses normal suspicions about the intentions of a man but has a deeper insight as well:

I go out to a party dressed to kill. I spend hours getting ready and when I get there I feel the ugliest person in the room. I like to receive attention but when it comes my way I just can't accept it. If a man comes up to me and says something nice I blush and immediately my mind is racing away. 'He wants something. Sex, of course, they all want it.' I know this is silly because in the end it is up to me whether he gets sex or not so there is no harm in his trying. But often I am wrong. No suggestion is made to me; they just want to say something nice and I want to run and hide myself. And yet the silly thing is that I am dolled up to get exactly what is given, attention. I feel they got it wrong, it's not me they are talking about.

But people are not always nice and unpleasant remarks are exchanged. The shy, diffident man or woman, who has actually managed to get close enough to make contact with others, hasn't much room to manoeuvre in if they are in fact criticized. If they have always been subjected to criticism and are particularly sensitive to it, as soon as they get a whiff of it, real or imaginary, they over-react and rapidly withdraw or create a scene.

The tendency to shyness and aloofness, coupled with oversensitivity to criticism or rejection, act as barriers to the openness and communication needed in ordinary human associations. If, in addition to such vulnerable tendencies, a person's previous experience is heavily marked with insecurity through frequent losses or unstable personal relationships – particularly with the parents – we have the psychological vignette of those who cannot cope with the processes of socialization without assistance.

So far two features have been described that are a helpful guide in the indications for seeking help. The first can be summarized as the accumulation of personal factors, coupled with experiences in childhood, which makes access to others difficult and drives the person into himself. Such a combination leads to social isolation, makes a person excessively vulnerable to loss and criticism, making it difficult to overcome the inevitable hurdles of transition, growth and adversity in life. One or an accumulation of stressful events plunges him into a reactive depression from which he cannot extricate himself without the intervention of another person. This other person is usually a relative or friend but sometimes he may need counselling or professional expertise to penetrate the sense of depression.

The second is the extension of the depressive mood in intensity and range of manifestations. Here the dividing line between depression as a normal reaction to stress and depression as an illness becomes clearer.

Details were given in Chapter II of the concept of depression as an illness which is characterized by a cluster of symptoms. These symptoms involve the mood itself, disturbance of sleep, loss of energy, appetite, weight, concentration, attention, anxiety and tension and, ultimately, the severe manifestations of delusional guilt and hallucinations.

It is in the presence, persistence and severity of these manifestations that the most certain indications for help lie. When a person finds himself or herself increasingly in the grip of such symptoms, week after week, with no signs of a let up, in fact the opposite – a gradual deterioration – then clearly the depression has moved into the category of illness which he can no longer control and which needs medical intervention.

This picture of illness may emerge out of the blue, be drifted into after weeks, months or years of normal and controlled anxiety or mild depressive features, so that a serious depressive illness may supervene on an inner state to which people have been habituated and accustomed for a long time. The additional stress may arise from a wide range of events such as family conflict, a bereavement, moving from one district to another, some personal reversal at work or in business, an illness, of which those of virus origin like 'flu, glandular fever, shingles, infection of the liver called hepatitis, or an operation are common triggering mechanisms. When a depressive illness is present which has replaced many years of mild anxiety or depressive reaction, it is far more difficult to recognize the need for help.

There is a third feature which should act as a warning signal that help is needed. The first is the inability to handle or break through after persistent efforts, human situations which others can manage with reasonable ease. The second is the engulfment of oneself into several and severe symptoms which are making ordinary living increasingly difficult and gradually grind one to a halt. The third is the suicidal feeling.

The thought that life is too dreadful to go on living

crosses the minds both of those who are miserable due to their life situation and of those who have crossed over to the state of depressive illness. In the midst of the various causes of acute unhappiness the desire for relief by ceasing to be is not by itself an unreasonable or surprising reaction. But these thoughts do no more than express a wish for relief; they do not carry any serious intent and the prospect of actually carrying out a suicidal act never seriously enters into the head of the person.

At some moment, however, the real possibility of the removal of oneself occurs to one. From the moment that the act of self-destruction is seriously contemplated as a way out of the predicament, we have the third serious reason for seeking help, particularly as the act itself may be carried out impulsively. Such a person, or those to whom this information has been communicated, should ensure that help is sought without further delay.

To sum up: there can never be an exact moment or indication for seeking help in the state of depression. No one, other than the individual concerned, can decide what degree of suffering he is prepared to undergo. There are even those who claim that, if a person wishes to destroy himself, that is his ultimate right and no one should interfere. Help should only be given to those who seek it.

Much as one wishes to preserve the complete freedom and choice of the individual, I am undoubtedly committed to the view that in certain circumstances, (when a person has reached a degree of depression where he is in serious danger of destroying himself or others) then help should be given. It should be given first on a voluntary basis and, if the person refuses this, by compulsory but temporary deprivation of freedom by being placed in a hospital. Though this view may not have universal acceptance (see the work of the American psychiatrist Professor Thomas Szaz) it does represent the consensus of opinion of the majority of psychiatrists.

This situation, however, is a rarity, in that the majority of depressed patients receive treatment in and out of hospital on a voluntary basis. By mentioning hospitals and doctors several hurdles have been jumped because we are assuming that the doctor is the first person to whom we turn for help.

Normally this is the case but it need not be necessarily so. People may turn for help to other agencies such as the Samaritans (see Chapter XIX), a clergyman, the police or any other readily available agency. But before people turn to professional help, they try to help themselves. In fact most transient depressions lift without professional intervention.

Here the question remains – how is this to be done? There is no simple answer. People devise a great range of individual answers which can be divided into those which can be carried out alone, those that involve others and those which are a combination of the two.

Those who like to conquer their depressive mood alone may overcome it with activity. They will forget their misery by doing something. They plunge more deeply into their work, they undertake new commitments. They carry out the age-old maxim of turning away from themselves and considering others. In the home there is always something which needs doing, such as decorating, repairing or constructing something new. The pleasure of achievement overcomes the distress or misery.

An essential element of depression is a sense of loss, of deprivation which can be compensated by some personal indulgence. Resorting to food, particularly attractive morsels or chocolates, is a well-tried remedy which brings, of course, its own curse of weight increase. Others resort to drink although alcohol can in fact, after an initial soothing sensation, deepen the depressive mood. Music can be a powerful mood elevator and, if it is associated with a crowd and dancing, the company of others has an added value. For some, their own uninterrupted company with a book, a warm bath or a walk are their special remedies.

For others company is essential and the mood does not change unless they find a comforting audience. This can be their spouse, parent, friend or, indeed, any caring listener. The tremendous work of the Samaritans is precisely their availability as a caring and attentive listener for as long as their client needs it. There are those who need more than one sympathetic listener; they need an audience. Their mood lifts when they are being paid attention by an appreciative gathering. Thus the need to communicate, to be understood, to be received, to be accepted, to feel we matter to one or more person is the common factor in all these situations.

Often the depression is accounted for by a clear event, a death, a failure, or a disappointment and time is the only healer. Other depressive episodes occur when we have hurt or damaged anyone, but particularly those we love, and relief only comes when we have had a chance to apologise, make suitable reparation and feel forgiven.

This event can also be an urgently needed material relief. A good deal of the ordinary everyday work of doctors, social workers and other professional agencies is providing material or psychological relief. Advice with regard to bad housing, financial difficulties, unemployment, unsuitable work, care for children when parents are indisposed, the relief of loneliness for the sick or the elderly, all these contribute a great deal to the relief of depressive reaction.

As already suggested, healing can be accelerated by talking about a problem, particularly when there is nothing more that can be done practically; this is a form of treatment to which we shall return in Chapter XV. Sometimes, though perhaps less nowadays than before, relief is sought from religion, talking to a priest or in the presence of a group of similarly religious-minded persons or going to confession. Seeking forgiveness from God is a common way of lifting a depressive reaction.

For those who are basically lonely and need companionship, then finding a friend, a girl-friend, a boy-friend or friendship in general is an effective answer. Initiating and maintaining a friendship can be seen as real acceptance of self, a success which others seek at work, in their social life, in creative enterprises or achievement in general, all of which can dispel a depressive mood.

Finally, depressive moods come and go frequently for no reason at all, and the person becomes gradually accustomed to such a pattern which persists for several years. There are as many ways of dealing with depression as there are individuals who experience it.

There remain those who need help from a doctor. Statistically they are about 10 per cent, a fact however which is of no value whatsoever to the individual except to be reassured that he is not the first nor the last person in the world to seek help and therefore need not feel ashamed or embarrassed to do so. We can next look at the likely forms of help that the doctor offers and how they work out in practice. In this chapter we have looked at the management of depression; in the next two we shall look at its treatment.

XIV The Treatment of Depression by Physical Means

In order to appreciate the great advances made in the treatment of depression recently, it is interesting to give a brief historical survey of the treatment of the mentally ill.

The history of all ancient civilizations contains references to and descriptions of mental disorders. With a few exceptions, such as the observations of Hippocrates (460-377 BC) and his school, the manifestations of mental illness were inextricably related to religion, mystical hypotheses, and both physical and psychological disturbances were related to sin and its appropriate expiation.

Such an approach meant that the mentally ill were treated as objects of fear and awe and, as is not uncommon in society, were made the scapegoats of its recurrent collective anxieties. For a time in the Middle Ages witches, most of whom were undoubtedly suffering from mental disorder, received the full brunt of society's displeasure and were physically tortured, burned and hanged.

But, if the fate of the mentally ill was not death or chains, flogging and ill-treatment remained generally their lot with few exceptions until the eighteenth century with the beginnings of humanitarian care. The reformers were the French doctor, Philippe Pinel (1745-1826) in France and William Tuke (1732-1822) in Britain.

Pinel obtained his medical degree in 1773 and wrote – 'The mentally ill, far from being guilty persons who merit punishment, are sick people whose miserable state deserves all the considerations due to suffering humanity.' In this country William Tuke set up the Retreat in York in 1796, an asylum to care for the mentally sick, with the assistance of the Society of Friends.

And so the modern era of care, respect, adequate nutrition and the diminution of cruelty for the mentally ill began.

But even so, fear receded only gradually and the fortunes of the mentally ill still fluctuated. Society remained cautious and towards the turn of the nineteenth century decided to retain its humanitarian approach but to place the mentally ill together in large institutions on the outskirts of cities where they remained isolated, out of sight and often out of reach of their relatives. These institutions, the mental hospitals of our day, have housed the sick for nearly a hundred years. Some of them have populations of a few hundred, others approaching the two thousand mark.

In the last twenty years there has been a further development in the policy of care which aims to treat psychological disorder in the general hospital, now called the district hospital, so that the distinction between physical and mental illness – with all the overtones of first and second class categories of illness citizenship – is gradually removed. It has become the policy of successive governments to build psychiatric units in general hospitals which, with outpatient facilities, will treat all psychiatric illness. No one argues that this is the right progression for acute psychiatric illness, although there is still a case to be made for retaining some aspects of the traditional mental hospital for those who need longer treatment.

The word treatment brings me back to the issue of what type of treatment was available to those who had to be hospitalized for their depression. The answer is that until the 1930s there was very little that could be considered specific. Careful studies had delineated the two main categories of severe mental illnesses, the affective disorders – of which depression was the main one – and the schizophrenias, but there was no breakthrough in treatment. Depressed patients were admitted to hospital and were placed in rows and rows of beds. The responsibility of the attendants was to feed them (no easy task when appetite is absent), make sure that they did not succumb to other complications – such as infections or tuberculosis – protect them from self-destructive impulses and wait. It is calculated that the natural history of a straightforward severe depressive illness was of the order of six to nine months before the depressive mood lifted slowly and spontaneously. There was nothing

D   F to do except hope and wait, a task that did not exactly encourage doctors to join the speciality or nurses to undertake the heavy responsibilities of caring. Many of these men and women from the ranks of both professions have retired, or are now retiring, and the country, which is ever ready (rightly) to fire its guns when a scandal is uncovered in one of the institutions, has appreciated too little the endeavours – particularly of the nursing staff – and their devoted work during these years when there was little to do except sustain hope. Some of this hope was soon to be translated into therapeutic intervention which produced dramatic results and which brings the account up to date.

The two forms of therapy which revolutionized the treatment of the depressive illnesses were, first, the introduction of electroconvulsive therapy and, secondly, in the last two decades, the arrival of a number of drugs collectively known as antidepressants which have the specific ability to change the mood and restore it to normal levels. Between them, electroconvulsive therapy (to be called ECT henceforth) and antidepressants have, in appropriate patients, cut down the course of an illness from months to a matter of three to four weeks. This unfortunately does not apply to everyone who reaches the stage of seeking help and the present challenge in clinical practice is in the evaluation of the patient's story so that the appropriate treatment is initiated. Much is common knowledge and widely practised, some is controversial and some the concern of current research and careful evaluation. In what follows no attempt is made to be comprehensive or unduly detailed by specifying individual drugs and forms of treatment or to pretend that a self-service advice column is possible. The ultimate responsibility remains in the hands of individual doctors who, together with their patients, must construct a course of action which is effective in individual circumstances.

Enough has been described of the wide variety of manifestations of the condition for it to be clear by now that there is no absolute right or wrong approach. On the other hand, there are now three decades of accumulated clinical experience which form the basis of a rational approach to treatment. This will be divided into two categories; the treatment of the less severe and the severe forms of depression or, in the realm of classification, the 'reactive' and 'endogenous' variety, bearing in mind that these labels are controversial and remain provisional.

REACTIVE DEPRESSION

By far the more likely reason for seeking help is the presence of a reactive form of depression, that is to say one in which – in addition to the depressed mood with or without weeping – the person will be experiencing marked symptoms of tension, anxiety, bodily aches and pains, disturbed sleep, have fears of fainting, going mad, losing control and exhaustion.

This is a group of symptoms that frequently arise from a stressful event and, in due course, will abate in most instances of their own accord. Thus many people will not seek help for them and will find that the discomfort will recede spontaneously. Many who do not like going to doctors for fear of troubling them and do not like to admit there is anything wrong with them, want to fight their own battles alone. They would consider going to a doctor a sign of weakness, are afraid that they will discover something terrible about their sanity, do not want to give their spouse or other members of the family an excuse for criticism or laughing at them, believe that they will prejudice their future or career and, for many other reasons, will wish to persevere on their own; and the vast majority will succeed.

Others will go to their doctor for a physical check up and when this gives them, in the overwhelming majority of cases, a clean bill of health, they will be left with a label which could be simply – 'It's your nerves' or 'You are just a bit anxious'. This will be tied up with some particular stress, physical (illness) or psychosocial of the types described in this book, or the actual diagnosis of depression will be given. And then what happens?

The matter can rest there because the reassurance derived from the examination, the absence of any dreaded revelation and the knowledge that the condition is self-limiting and will clear up may be enough. Or this particular doctor-patient relationship may recognize and face together the special stress in the life of the patient so that the strength acquired by the patient from this combined approach is enough. This strength, incidentally, can be derived, after the initial reassurance from doctor, through husband, wife, relatives, friends, pastor, counsellor, social worker – anyone who is in fact prepared to share the period of distress. Of course, rarely, there may not be anybody else other than the doctor, although increasingly there are voluntary organizations who offer precisely this form of help; the role of the Samaritans, for example, will be considered in Chapter XIX.

But, if befriending is not enough, is there any place for medication? The patient will seek relief for persistent and unbearable symptoms of fears, tension, disturbed sleep and the mood itself and each of these manifestations can be helped.

A great number of minor tranquillizers exist which, given at any time during the day, ease the tension and anxiety manifestations. Some of them are given during the day or at night and, having sedative or hypnotic-like properties, will actually improve the sleep as well. So, for some who require medicines, this need not be more than the use of a minor tranquillizer. But for others more is needed and here there is the next step in treatment, namely the use of an antidepressant. This is where the breakthrough in treatment has taken place because there is a wide variety of antidepressants which the family doctor can prescribe, so the patient does not need, in the majority of instances, even to see a specialist in a hospital. This revolution is about twenty years old and marks a minor but distinctive achievement which, if not exactly comparable to the arrival of antibiotics, in the control of infection, has given equally as much relief from suffering.

The exact choice, amount and duration is a matter for the doctor to decide and will not be considered here any further. What will be considered are the main differences between the two groups of antidepressants and some of the current opinions about their indications.

It is the opinion of many workers that the monoxidase

inhibitor group of antidepressants are particularly useful in the group of depressions under consideration in which anxiety and tension is predominant. This is the type of depression called 'reactive'.[1]

The history of this group of drugs, it will be remembered, started when a drug (Iproniazid) found to be useful in the treatment of tuberculosis was also noted to cause euphoria in some of the patients. This chance finding led to its development and the whole family of these antidepressants was introduced.

In Chapter IV it was mentioned that monoamines were an important element in normal functioning of the brain, and related to the control of mood. The monoamine oxidase inhibitors act by inhibiting a substance (enzyme) which destroys the monoamines when released in their cell. By inhibiting the action of the enzyme, there is a build up of the monoamines with corresponding lifting of the depressive mood.

Patients will know when they are on such antidepressants because they will be asked to observe certain dietary restrictions. They will be asked not to eat such food items as cheese, Marmite, Bovril, broad beans and other items (they should follow carefully the list given to them), nor to drink alcohol. There are many reasons for this, but it is mainly due to the sudden rise of blood pressure which gives a severe headache and may occasionally be dangerous. The drugs inhibit the monoamine oxidase which in turn allows for an accumulation of monoamine and, since these foods contain also special monoamines (tyramine), together they can cause a build-up of monoamines and this unwanted rise in blood pressure.[2] Since these observations were made, and care has been taken to warn patients of the need to heed the dietary precautions, these side effects have been virtually eliminated. Thus, when there are good medical reasons for taking these medicines, they are prescribed with the certainty that, provided the diet is adhered to, there are no grounds for withholding their undoubted benefits.

One of the snags with antidepressant treatment is that patients do not go on taking their tablets. There are several reason for this, one of which is that the relief does not begin to show itself for about ten to fifteen days and, in the absence of immediate results, they are abandoned. This applies even more in the case of the tricyclic group to be discussed next. But even when patients persevere, which is the only way to get the benefit, they may experience side effects of the medicines which put them off.

A side effect is a symptom produced by the tablet which is not dangerous but unpleasant. Most side effects tend to get better after a short time but sometimes they are a nuisance which discourages the continuation of the treatment. The monoamine oxidase inhibitors may cause dizziness, feelings of weakness when getting up from the lying or sitting position, dry mouth, constipation, delayed micturition and, in the male, ejaculative difficulties or, more rarely, impotence and increased weight by retention of water. None of these is serious and, if the patient is prepared for the possibility (they do not invariably occur) and provided the advantages outweigh the disadvantages, the medication is persisted with.

ENDOGENOUS DEPRESSION

So far the treatment described is conducted at the level of the doctor's surgery or outpatient clinic of a general hospital. Before the advent of this medication, some patients would have already needed hospitalization and certainly this would have been the case in the group described below, the severe or endogenous group of depression. The depression is marked, sustained and is accompanied by loss of sleep, appetite, weight, libido, inability to concentrate, failing memory, guilt feelings, delusions and hallucinations with the distinct possibility of suicide.

Here we are in the realms of a serious condition which demands medical treatment as a matter of urgency because a life is at stake. If the patient seeks help he will of course receive it but sometimes the relatives or friends recognize that something is seriously amiss before the patient does and have to initiate the call for help which in this instance must be medical.

What help is available? Before the modern era of anti-depressants, such a condition almost invariably required hospitalization. Now an attempt can be made, and often is made, to treat all but those who would clearly be a danger to themselves, by the use of antidepressants, thus keeping the patient at home. It is only when this line of treatment does not work, for one reason or another, that hospitalization is indicated.

The patient will need relief for his mood, insomnia, lethargy and sheer inability to function, all of which are brought out in a fictional but authentic account of the depressed state.

I have never in my life had insomnia before this summer, and this isn't even normal insomnia, coming as it does at the tail end of the night or beginning of the morning. It's sheer hell, and it's always the same. It always happens on a night when I've fallen asleep without trouble, helped by pills or not, and I sleep soundly until 2, 3, 4 a.m. when I suddenly wake up – Bang – with the whole syndrome – the cold sweat, my heart is racing, my pyjamas are stuck to me with a cold sweat, etc. As I lie there breathing hard, unknotting my hands, wondering what woke me up, the Guilt and Shame hits me like a ton of bricks – Guilt and Shame without any rational focus, which of course is the worst part of it. Just what in God's name have you done to make yourself feel so stupid and worthless and terrible? I ask myself. You have not been unfaithful to Jonathan, you haven't stolen or cheated or murdered or been cruel. What is it? And then slowly, by way of answering, the little review begins.

At first it's Humiliating Moments and Wicked Deeds from childhood: the time I wet my pants in first grade: the time I stole a manicure set from the 5 and 10 and the manager collared me . . . On and on it goes, making me toss and writhe in bed, until the parade of objects begins.

I see tarnished flatware and streaky windows: I see burnt-out light bulbs, cracked cups and saucers and

dinner plates and unwaxed floors; I see shirts and
pyjamas without buttons, shoes that need re-heeling,
shoes without laces, socks with holes in the toes, worn
thin sheets, squeezed-out tubes of toothpaste, slivers of
soap, a toaster with a dangerous frayed cord, an iron with
a broken plug . . .

I gave up and lit a cigarette and by the flare of the
match saw it was quarter past four . . .[3]

A night like this, followed by a day of utter weariness,
week after week, leads to total exhaustion and the need for
treatment.

The first line of treatment here is the immediate introduction of antidepressants, this time the variety known as the
tricyclic group. Unlike the monoamine inhibitors which
inhibit the metabolism of monamines inside the cell, the
tricyclic group act by inhibiting the re-uptake of the amine,
noradrenaline, just outside the cell and so it is left to act
for a much longer period.

These medicines, with or without night sedation, also
take ten to fifteen days to begin to work and also have
side effects. In a study of 260 patients having such medicine,
15.4 per cent had side effects. The main group of these
consisted of sixteen who complained of drowsiness, eight
further agitation and confusion, seven of dry mouth, difficulties with voiding, with vision and palpitations. No one
who was free of serious physical illness had any dangerous
complications. These medicines are therefore extremely safe
when used in their proper amounts and under medical supervision.[4]

Antidepressants are highly effective but patients give up
taking them. In one study 40 per cent did not take the
prescribed drugs.[5] The reason for this may be side effects,
the sheer task of remembering or complicated personal
feelings which make a person not want to rely on drugs
which they fear. 'I don't want to rely on drugs'; 'I don't
want to get hooked on them'; 'I don't believe in tablets' are
common excuses. Some of these difficulties are being overcome by reducing the number of tablets required or by
taking all the required amount at night and so avoiding any

side effects or interference with work during the day.

Provided that the treatment is successful, how long should it be continued? There are not definite answers to this question but a period of at least six months and probably a year is considered necessary at present.[6]

If antidepressant therapy does not work, then resort is made for the severe cases to ECT. No one knows exactly how ECT works but it remains the standby of treatment in all severe cases or in those in which antidepressants are not sufficient. Since the introduction of antidepressants there has nevertheless been a considerable reduction in its use. ECT is usually given in hospital as an inpatient treatment but sometimes psychiatric units arrange for outpatient ECT.

In ECT a small amount of electricity passes through the brain and produces a convulsion. This convulsion, on which its effectiveness depends, is repeated usually on six occasions over a period of two to three weeks but more can be given if necessary. The patient is treated as if he was going to have an operation; that is to say, is advised not to take anything by mouth from the midnight before. After a suitable preparation before the treatment, an injection is given to anaesthetize and give complete muscle relaxation, which in fact means the patient feels absolutely nothing, the treatment is given, which is all over in minutes. It is a treatment which is extremely safe and, if proper selection is made of the severe depression, the results are excellent. The only side effect following ECT is a memory disturbance which is short lived and leaves no enduring deficit. Thus there is no reason whatsoever of being frightened of this treatment when it is recommended.

The other major condition related to depression is its opposite mania and here there have also been recently major advances with the use of the drug lithium as a long term protective agent which cuts down the number of attacks. Lithium has also been recently used to reduce recurrent attacks of depression.

Apart from antidepressants, tranquillisers, ECT and, extremely rarely, leucotomy, female hormones and antidiuretics are occasionally used to relieve premenstrual symptoms or some of the worst features of the menopause.

In a matter of some thirty years – but particularly in the last decade – the whole nature of the treatment of depression has been transformed and we can look forward to further advances in the future. There are still patients who present exceptional difficulties but they get fewer and fewer and so everyone, patients and relatives, can look increasingly with hope for the relief of their symptoms. But until the arrival of ECT and antidepressants, the only alternative was the talking therapy, psychotherapy or psychoanalysis. Some doctors feel that there is little room for this approach nowadays and this subject is considered in the next and final chapter on treatment.

Notes

1. Sargant, W., Dally, P., (1962), 'Treatment of Anxiety States by Antidepressant Drugs', *British Medical Journal*, I:6
2. Blackwell, B., Price, J., Taylor, D., (1967), 'Hypertensive Interactions between monoamine oxidase inhibitors and foodstuffs', *British Journal of Psychiatry* 113:497
3. Kaufman, S., (1967), *Diary of a Mad Housewife*, Michael Joseph, London
4. Occasional Survey, (1972), 'Adverse Reactions to the Tricyclic-Antidepressant Drugs', *Lancet*: 529
5. Willcox, D. R. G., Gillan, R., Hare, E. H., (1965), *British Medical Journal*, II, 790
6. *Lancet*, (1972), Annotation: 'Management of a Depressive Illness', 21 October, 1972

XV The Treatment of Depression by Psychotherapy

The argument concerning the usefulness of psychotherapy varies from country to country and from psychiatrist to psychiatrist and a brief explanation of the reasons for this is necessary.

Breuer and Freud published in 1893 their observations in a study called 'On the Psychical Mechanism of Hysterical Phenomena: Preliminary Communication', in which they described the beginnings of the talking therapy.[1] Essentially what this paper suggested was that physical symptoms, which were hysterical in nature, were capable of removal if the emotions which triggered them off were released by talking about them. Breuer withdrew from this research but Freud went on and psychoanalysis was born.

Psychoanalysis gradually became a technique by which a person is helped to reach unconscious feelings linked with events which, because of their painful nature, were repressed. This repression meant that a quantity of energy, emotional in nature, existed and maintained symptoms which are physical or psychological in nature. If the feeling or the affect could be released by putting it into words, it had a beneficial effect. This simplistic view developed step by step into a complicated system of therapy which changed the face of psychological treatment.

Since Freud, psychiatrists have divided themselves into those who have followed the principles of dynamic psychology and its therapy as the first line of attack of psychological problems and those who, while recognizing their significance, have not used its therapeutic principles except in a secondary capacity, if at all. This latter group have tended to resort to physical forms of treatment as their primary therapy. With the arrival of the extensive range of antidepressant and other drugs, the question now remains whether there is any justification for psychoanalysis and its derivatives psychotherapy and group psychotherapy, in the treatment o depression. In answering this question certain principles ar beyond controversy.

First no one, not even Freud himself, ever seriously sug gested that psychoanalysis is the appropriate form of treat ment for the severe, psychotic or endogenous form of depres sion. The nature of the condition precludes the use o orthodox psychoanalytic techniques which require that th patient should be able to transfer feelings originally ex perienced in one situation through one person, usually parental figure, on to the therapist and relive them wit him. The severely depressed patient withdraws into himsel and is incapable of this transference. Such an illness, anyon would agree, should be treated with the appropriate physica form of therapy.

At the other end of the scale, transient and not sever forms of depression which are self-limiting are not usuall considered worthy of psychotherapeutic treatment, nor ar those which are clearly accounted for by a precipitating event such as the loss of a loved one. It is exceptional to conside psychotherapy in these circumstances.

This leaves the less severe, 'reactive', 'neurotic' group o depressive conditions. Since these conditions are ofte associated with a great deal of anxiety, there is nowaday a very good case to be made for using the tranquillizin group of drugs to suppress the manifestations.

It would appear, therefore, that there are no indications fo the psychoanalytic approach in depressive disorders an some, though not all psychiatrists would adopt this position Furthermore, a review of research findings in psychotherap does not show in any clear manner its therapeutic value.[2] I is fair to say that there are very few sophisticated researc studies of these techniques sensitive enough to assess th complex nature of change involved in the process of psycho therapy.

Despite the absence of any precise proof of the value o dynamic therapy, there undoubtedly remain psychiatrists o both sides of the Atlantic – although many more in USA tha in Britain – who would insist that there is a place for it

Individual therapists will quote their own experience of undoubted benefit to patients although even here there is a danger that the results obtained depend on the self-limiting spontaneous remission of the condition, rather than the specific influence of therapy. This still does not detract from the relief that the patient derives in the course of therapy and for some this may make the difference between life and death.

But ultimately, if there is a rationale for psychotherapy, it is to be found somewhere else; namely in those patients whose personality causes a persistent inability to cope with aspects of themselves or their relationships with others, so that they find themselves in recurrent stressful situations which trigger off severe and persistent depressive reactions.

Psychoanalysis, or its derivatives, is now primarily directed at helping the growth of the personality which has a secondary and indirect result of reducing the conflict situation that precipitates the depressive mood.

Even in these circumstances it is important to put this treatment in perspective. Psychotherapeutic treatment in all its forms is time consuming and requires persistence and hard work on the part of the patient. There are few therapists, the facilities in the National Health Service are extremely limited and therefore inevitably only a certain amount is done under its aegis, the rest being carried out under the private sector. The private sector tends to be concentrated in the big cities, so that this form of therapy raises not only basic scientific questions but has a marked scarcity; thus it requires the most careful evaluation before it is applied.

Nevertheless, even if formal psychotherapy has strictly limited application for depression, there can be little doubt that the alleviation of depression entirely through the dispensing of pills without letting the patient express some of his or her feelings, is unlikely ever to be the right answer. Even if ultimately drugs do successfully treat all forms of depression, pills are not handed over to 'cases' but to people and these people have feelings which need to be listened and responded to. The only enemy here is time and, even if it provides a legitimate excuse for all doctors, good treatment ultimately requires a dialogue – however short – between two people, the doctor and the patient.

Far more often what is needed is not formal psycho-therapy but an opportunity for patients to express some of their pent-up feelings of a distress situation, which can be an enormous source of relief. Increasingly, the badly needed time for such exchange is found, not between doctor and patient, but between the patient and voluntary workers, such as the Samaritans, (see Chapter XIX) who are able to provide the time for this exchange.

But, for some patients with protracted, lifelong personality difficulties associated with depression, some form of psycho-therapy is essential. Here is the extended account of the experience of a housewife. She had recurrent bouts of depression, had entertained suicidal intentions and, although medication relieved some of her symptoms, she needed to discover the reasons and understand more fully her dis-ability. Without much faith in the process, she nevertheless decided to join a group, which is one form of psychotherapy.

Long periods of unrelieved depression had an insidious effect on me which made me increasingly vulnerable to stress and the resulting tensions. Barely aware that I was gradually losing contact with reality, self-blame and hopelessness had imperceptibly become what I considered to be a normal state of feeling. Self-destructive impulses, although frightening, were felt to be reasonable. In-creasing isolation from people and activities, and the blunting of positive and constructive ways of behaving became an established way of life even when the depres-sion lifted temporarily. When the periods of bearable life between attacks of depression began to grow shorter, I began to sink into a state of hopelessness. Depression became more intense, lasted longer and suicide became a permanent and much-dwelt on possibility, an inevitable event which could not be escaped. Tension and irritability mounted unseen and almost unfelt until a slight frustration would trigger off an explosion which ended in havoc around me. I felt so violent that it ceased to matter who or what received the force of it – family, friends, relations and even total strangers; the house and garden came to resemble a battlefield. Although I felt that I didn't care any more, I did care, deeply. I felt completely trapped because the whole situation had become a vicious circle. I felt that I was a bad person and, when the badness erupted and caused hurt to others, then the badness was proved repeatedly to exist. This proof always increased the helplessness and accelerated despair. There was no way out of the circle, and that knowledge alone brought about an increase in depression. Suicide alone remained the answer; it was a practical solution to a problem. I was a damaging person, and the person and the damage to others would cease.

I had grown weary of pinning my hope on drugs. Beginning at school and continuing intermittently, various drugs and combinations of drugs had been taken. Some symptoms were suppressed, but I always ended up back at the beginning.

It was when I finally realized that nothing was ever going to change that I became desperate enough to seek further help. Desperate, but not hopeful. After all, it had been going on for nearly ten years, and before that in a less severe way for more than ten years. I had no faith in doctors, didn't trust them and didn't intend to start doing so.

When psychotherapy was proposed, I felt cheated and let down, especially after the purpose and manner of it had been outlined. All I wanted was to get better, and it sounded a waste of time and effort. I felt too ill to be bothered to try it. I had hoped that ECT would be proposed; it sounded drastic enough to do something, no matter what. When it was explained repeatedly that physical treatment would not remove the cause but merely alleviate the symptoms, I became deeply suspicious and openly hostile. Someone was pulling a fast one on me. When I was eventually told that the psychotherapy envisaged was group therapy, I was very angry. This was the last straw. Having with difficulty managed to talk to one person, to be told next to talk to a group of strangers, was more than I could stomach. But it was the first time I had received what seemed like real help;

I had my back against the wall, and presumed this to mean about six months. I wanted results and short cuts, and six months didn't sound short.

I was deeply suspicious of the therapist and his motives for doing this work. Either it was just a job, or an exeriment or a gimmick – either way I refused to believe that the care – apparently real – was genuine. There had to be a catch in it somewhere.

I had always been independent and self-sufficient, and bitterly resented what I took to be an attempt to make me dependent. The possibility that I was being helped to real independence never occurred to me. That I had always been a prisoner of my own inherited and acquired handicaps I knew quite well. But the possibility of any of this being changed was ridiculous and very far-fetched. The others in the group had various problems, all severe, all long standing and, as far as I could gather, intractable. We were a very mixed bunch of people, but we did have one thing in common. We were all sceptical. No one initially had any faith in what was going on, or in the person who was so confident in their ability to help.

The problems of the others appalled me. I wanted to help them and did not know where to start. When it was pointed out to me firmly and frequently that my first priority was myself, real resistance began to show. This was a point of view I simply could not accept. The idea of learning how to accept care before I could give any to others was alien to my way of thinking. The gradual realization that I had many needs, pointed out on numerous occasions, stirred up enormous anger which bewildered me by taking different directions. I was angry that my needs became so obvious that denying them was a waste of time; angry at everyone being so patient and accepting – I did not want to be at the receiving end of their charity; worst of all, my anger took the familiar turn inwards at being completely unable to receive what was being offered.

I had a view of myself which was considered to be faulty and distorted. Feeling that this was not the case I strove to be what I thought was honest. Frustration mounted when no one appeared prepared to accept what I felt was the true picture. After all, I knew myself very well, and what I knew was hated with destructive vengeance. The affection, patience and understanding bounced off week after week. I longed for people to stop trying to reach me; it was all such a waste of their time. It all sounded good in theory; perhaps it would work for others; I never seemed to make much progress. When depressed I was usually unable to speak at all, and resented the impossibility of finding words to express my feelings. Feelings caused havoc, but could not be articulated. The exhibition of infantile traits in the group became something to be dreaded. Aggression, jealousy, inferiority feelings, attention-seeking behaviour, sullen silences and periods of helpless weeping punctuated the group sessions. No one minded. No one sat in judgment or criticized or told me to pull myself together. I felt that they ought to. The tolerance being shown was too great to be genuine. I was being asked to trust other people's feelings about me, and I was too fearful and too cynical to trust anyone at that time.

Although needing to talk, I didn't want to. It brought the painful feelings I had about myself out into the open. They were painful enough shut away, but I could not bear to face them and certainly not share them with others. If I did manage to talk for a few minutes, guilt overwhelmed me at feeling that I had taken up the whole hour. Perception of what actually took place took a very long time to achieve. My own feelings distorted everything. Coming to terms with guilt was the most difficult part of the whole long process. Having always felt to blame when things went wrong, this was a most difficult thing to relinquish. The worst aspect was the feeling that I was a damaging person when involved with others; being loved by me would inevitably damage or destroy them, or hurt them in some way.

Looking back, all this now seems so long ago. There was no definite point at which change took place. It was slow and frequently very painful. The indescribable pain of being depressed, isolated and suicidal was often felt to be preferable to the pain of being reached by others. The warm way in which others showed their regard for me was difficult to cope with. Progress was erratic. Sometimes one made great strides and the resulting feeling of well-being went on for weeks. At other times it ground to a halt and discouragement set in. Many times I left the group, determined never to return. But every inch of ground fought over and won was retained in spite of many setbacks. Dependency remained a problem for a long time. It was dreadful to find myself needing other people. Convinced that I could do it single-handed, I thought a good way to shorten the process would be to read everything available. This would enable me to gain insight and eliminate the apparent necessity of forming relationships and accepting help. My disappointment when this did not work was intense. The emotional insight I had gained certainly shed light on what I read, but it would not work the other way round. Not a scrap of emotional insight was achieved by reading. I had to learn again and again to my disgust that it only came from communicating with other human beings.

It was a confusing discovery to find that the others in the group were not repelled by my weaknesses and miseries. This meant yet another change in attitude to myself. Apparently I was always acceptable, whether frail or strong! Occasionally I began to feel that perhaps I was a good person; that I had gifts and abilities which could be used; that my effect on others was often far from destructive. As these feelings grew, the intense feelings of inferiority and inadequacy began to recede. The fleeting moments of feeling like this became longer periods of weeks, and even months sometimes. In proportion to this, the periods of being completely unable to cope, and being overwhelmed by the inevitability of it all, diminished also. Life became much more tolerable because the processes that went on between people were understood. It was a learning situation; perhaps more correctly a re-learning one. Faulty patterns of feelings, behaviour, attitude and response had to be re-learnt so that straightforward communication and relationship could take place without being distorted by fantasy and infantile reaction taking over.

Up to this time, I had been on the defensive against people. Because I did not like myself, I naturally expected others to feel the same way about me. To guard against the pain of experiencing this unsolicited, a way had to be found to cope with it. This I had achieved by anticipating it. Attack is always the best means of defence! To attack first by being aggressive became automatic, though often the aggression was neatly disguised, even into its opposite! It was a form of manipulation in which I did the manipulating! Usually people respond to aggression and hostility by being the same back again. When they did so, my deep fears were confirmed – I was not likable! What I had taken to be reality was exposed repeatedly as fantasy. This was to prove to be the great benefit of being in a group – a benefit very definitely unappreciated by me. You just cannot manipulate a group of people.

They kept on uncovering my knack of distorting all communication. They proved that silence was not weighty condemnation; that friendly remarks were not sarcasm, that patience and tolerance did not cover a whole-hearted desire to get rid of me. For a time, flippancy became a very useful defence. As long as I managed to turn the situation into a laugh-in, I could hope to keep it superficial. That never worked for long – someone always spotted what I was doing. More confusion and more anger.

The reduction of internal stress resulted in an enormous increase in ability to cope with external stress. Freedom to manoeuvre within difficult life situations started being taken for granted. I learnt what independence really meant – not being trapped helplessly by my own problems.

The richness of knowing other people, and being known by them, was a revelation to me. It became possible both to give and receive, and still feel good about it. When I witness others' scepticism and fear, and do not share it myself, I am able to realize how far I have travelled. Understanding only too well how they feel, one feels immense hope for them instead of frustration at being unable to help.

Sometimes the group sessions were tense, difficult, stationary. Often they were exhilarating and even hilarious. Usually they were slow and painful. They never for a moment became easy, for anyone.

Occasionally I become depressed, twice severely. This can be lived through now because my feelings about myself are so changed. What I have gained is permanent; there is energy and initiative available for intellectual and recreational pursuits and 90 per cent of the time I feel extremely well. Not the best wife and mother by any means, but not the worst either! Hope has become a reality which endures.

Whatever the form of psychotherapy, it is a process which, as she states, gives the patient a second opportunity to un-learn and re-learn new feelings about oneself and establish new relationships with others, and when this is essential for living then medication is not sufficient.

Notes

1. Breuer, J. and Freud, S., (1893), *Studies in Hysteria, Complete Psychoanalytical Works*, ed. J. Strachey, Vol. II, Hogarth Press, London
2. Rachman, S., (1971), *The Effects of Psychotherapy*, Pergamon Press, Oxford

XVI   History of Suicide

Temporary or sustained distress accompanying all forms of depression tends to find, in the absence of relief, one final answer in suicide. Depression is certainly the most common accompaniment and the background to all attempts at self-destruction. In the next two chapters, an account will be given of some of the current views on the subject of suicide which, on a conservative estimate, claims some 1000 lives every day throughout the world.

The beginning and conclusion of life are related to the mystery of creation itself and involve the most profound issues in evaluating its ultimate meaning. Life has value but by whom or how this value has been bestowed or emerged remains the controversy between those who are committed to a Creator God – who has ultimate control over all life – and those who see it as the process of evolution which can be explained by scientific knowledge.

Thus, while everyone will grant the intrinsic value of life, not everyone is likely to agree about its termination and the history of suicide can be expected to reflect this range of diversity. The act of suicide has been described primarily in relation to literature in A. Alvarez's book, *The Savage God*[1] and, in a more detailed scientific article, by Dr Rosen,[2] which was later incorporated into *A Handbook for the Study of Suicide*.[3]

Dr Rosen begins his article with the following words:

As a form of human behaviour, suicide is probably as ancient as man himself. Suicide has been practised for thousands of years in primitive and historic societies, but the ubiquity of the phenomenon has been associated with a wide diversity of attitude and feeling in the judgment of suicidal behaviour. Society's responses to the act of self-destruction can be viewed as a spectrum ranging from outright condemnation on the one hand, through mild disapproval to acceptance and incorporation into the socio-cultural system on the other. But just as societies vary in their reaction to suicide, so attitude within a society has changed in the course of time.[4]

It is this change in attitudes throughout history that will be examined in relation to its effect on Western society and particularly Britain.

The Greeks and Romans had a mixed approach to suicide. There were philosophical attitudes which supported and those which opposed it. The Stoics approved of it, following the example of their founder Zeno. According to him 'The wise man will for reasonable cause make his own exit from life on his country's behalf or for the sake of his friends, or if he suffer intolerable pain, mutilation or incurable disease.'[5] Both civilizations approved suicide for the sake of honour, to avoid capture, humiliation and shameful death and there were several instances of these. Epicureans opposed suicide and there were in fact practical measures taken to punish those who tried it. For example, in Athens it was customary to chop off the hand of a would-be suicide, if possible that with which he had attempted to take his life. In Rome those who hanged themselves were refused an honourable burial. But these deterrents lacked a deep religious or philosophical basis. They were practical measures against a tendency towards self-destruction which had assumed large-scale proportions in the Imperial period.

With the advent of Christianity, a more rigorous condemnation began to take shape, although its origins were not to be found in any precise directions in the Bible. There are five instances of suicide reported in the Old Testament and one in the New, that of Judas Iscariot. By the first century AD Josephus, faced with the inevitable defeat of his army by the Romans, considered the possibility of collective suicide but argued against it. 'For those who have laid mad hands upon themselves, the darker regions of the nether world receive their souls and God, their Father, visits upon their posterity the outrageous acts of the parents. That is why this crime, so hateful to God, is punished also by the sagest of legislators.'[6] But Josephus

supported the idea of protecting the Torah and therefore
suicide in defence of religion was allowed as, for example,
the mass suicide of the defenders of Masada.

But gradually the Christian opposition gained ground
and the final formulation was made by St Augustine in the
City of God. Augustine condemned suicide on three grounds.
It violated the Commandment – 'Thou shalt not Kill' which
applied to all innocent lives, one's own as much as another's;
it precluded any opportunity for repentance: and it was a
cowardly act. The only exception was for those who did so
under divine inspiration in the pursuit of protecting the
faith. With this view firmly established, synods and councils
promulgated the various punishments. Burial in consecrated
ground was refused and attempted suicide was punished by
exclusion from the fellowship of the Church for two months.

In the Middle Ages St Thomas Aquinas elaborated on
and supported further the position of Augustine and condemned suicide on the grounds that God alone has control
over life and death. In deciding the moment of his own death,
a suicide was usurping God's power. Echoing Aristotle, he
also condemned suicide as an offence against the community
by depriving it of one of its members. The Augustinian-
Thomist position generally remains that of Christianity to
this very day. Suicide is condemned as a violation of the
Fifth Commandment, as contrary to nature, an usurpation
of God's prerogative and a social wrong.[7]

Dante, writing in the *Inferno*, describes the wood which
encloses the souls of suicides. The soul of Piero delle Vigne,
Chancellor and chief adviser to the Emperor Frederick II,
accused of treason, disgraced and imprisoned, who killed
himself some sixteen years before Dante was born now
explains to Dante what happens to such a soul.

> When the wild soul leaps from the body,
> Which its own mad violence forces it to quit,
> Minos dispatches it down to the seventh ditch.
>
> It falls in the wood; no place is picked for it,
> But as chance carries it, there it falls to be,
> And where it falls, it sprouts like a corn of wheat.

And grows to a sapling, and thence to a wild tree;
Then the Harpies feed on its leaves, and the sharp bite
Gives agony, and a vent to agony.

When Dante touches the tree he is shattered by the
consequences.

So I put forth my hand a little way,
And broke a branchlet from a thorn-tree tall;
And the trunk cried out — 'Why tear my limbs away?'

There it grew dark with blood, and therewithal
Cried out again — 'Why dost thou rend my bones?
Breathes there no pity in thy breast at all?

'We that are turned to trees were human once;
Nay, thou shouldst tender a more pious hand
Though we had been the souls of scorpions.'

As, when you burn one end of a green brand
Sap at the other oozes from the wound,
Sizzling as the imprisoned airs expand.

So from that broken splint came words and blood
At once: I dropped the twig, and like to me
Rooted to the ground with terror, there I stood.[8]

This theological orientation, echoed in literature, begins
to slowly change from the time of the Renaissance.

John Donne wrote a book on the subject called *Biathan-
atos*[9] which was published posthumously in 1644. In it he
argues that suicide is not incompatible with the laws of God,
nature or reason. 'Methinks I have the keys of my prison
in mine own hand, and no remedy presents itself so soon to
my heart, as mine own sword.'[10]

Robert Burton is also more conciliating in his book *The
Anatomy of Melancholy* published in 1621. He describes the
distress leading to the suicide.

In such sort doth the torture and extremity of his misery
torment him, that he can take no pleasure in his life,

but is in a manner enforced to offer violence unto himself, to be freed from his present insufferable pains. So some (saith Fracastorius) in fury, but most in despair, sorrow, fear and out of the anguish and vexation of their souls, offer violence to themselves; for their life is unhappy and miserable . . . Thus of their goods and bodies we can dispose: but what shall become of their souls, God alone can tell . . . We ought not to be so rash and vigorous in our censures as some are, charity will judge and hope the best: God be merciful unto us all.[11]

The reference to goods and bodies reflects the penalties imposed on those who committed suicide by refusing them burial rites, burying the body in the highway and driving a stake through it as well as by forfeiture of land and goods.

From the seventeenth century onwards there was a continuing modification both in attitude and the rigour of the law. By the eighteenth century, the Age of Reason, Christian considerations were largely superseded by rational approaches. David Hume's attack on conventional morality on suicide appeared in 1777, the year after he died:

Were the disposal of human life so much reserved as the peculiar province of the Almighty that it were an encroachment on his right, for men to dispose of their own lives; it would be equally criminal to act for the preservation of life as for its destruction. If I turn aside a stone which is falling upon my head, I disturb the course of nature, and I invade the peculiar province of the Almighty by lengthening my life beyond the period which by the general laws of matter and motion he had assigned it.

A hair, a fly, an insect is able to destroy this mighty being whose life is of such importance. Is it an absurdity to suppose that human providence may dispose of what depends on such insignificant causes? It would be no crime indeed to divert the Nile or Danube from its course, were I able to effect such purpose. What then is the crime in turning a few ounces of blood from their natural channel?[12]

Attitudes softened in theory, practice lagged behind. It was not until 1823 that burial was allowed in a churchyard, and then only at night. Perhaps one of the reasons which delayed the modification of the law was the prevailing view in the eighteenth century that suicide was on the increase and that it was a particular English Malady. A British physician writing in 1733 agrees with this view in what is a classic of uninformed, unscientific 'common sense' dissertation not unlike those views which, in updated form, still grace innumerable 'authoritative' accounts on this and every other subject by those who think they have the complete answer to any human predicament. Writing on the English Malady he says:

> The title I have chosen for this treatise is a reproach universally thrown on this island by foreigners, and all our neighbours on the continent, by whom nervous distempers, spleen, vapours and lowness of spirits are in derision, called the English Malady. And I wish there were not so good grounds for this reflection. The moisture of our air, the variableness of our weather (from our situation amidst the ocean), the rankness and fertility of our soil, the richness and heaviness of our food, the wealth and abundance of the inhabitants (from their unusual trade), the inactivity and sedentary occupation of the better sort (among whom the evil mostly rages) and the horror of living in great, populous and consequently unhealthy towns, have brought forth a class and set up distemper, with atrocious and frightful symptoms, scarce known to our ancestors, and never rising to such fatal heights, nor affecting such numbers in any other known nation. These nervous disorders being computed to make almost one third of the complaints of the people of condition in England.[18]

Even though suicide was considered to be a national emergency in the eighteenth century proper investigations into incidence or causes did not begin until the nineteenth century and did not get into their stride until the twentieth. In the absence of accurate information, rumour or theory abounded. For example, many physicians considered it a disease in its own right characterized by a thickening of the skull.[14] But not everyone believed this and the modern view that suicidal behaviour is a symptom and not a disease of mental disorder was clearly stated by the famous French psychiatrist, Esquirol.[15]

As medical opinion on suicide changed, so did the view of writers and poets. First there was what Alvarez calls the Romantic state, which was suicidal. The Romantics linked together youth, poetry and death. Keats died in 1821 at the age of twenty-five; Shelley in 1822 at twenty-nine and Byron in 1824 at thirty-six, having remarked that: 'No man ever took a razor into his hand who did not at the same time think how easily he might sever the silver cord of life.' The Romantics, by the very nature of their writings, were obsessed by the subject of death and self-destruction.[16]

By the beginning of the twentieth century pragmatism was creeping in and one scene in Joyce's *Ulysses* reflects this through a conversation by four men on the way to a funeral.

'But the worst of all,' Mr Power said, 'is the man who takes his own life.' Martin Cunningham drew out his watch briskly, coughed and put it back. 'The greatest disgrace to have in the family,' Mr Power added. 'Temporary insanity, of course,' Martin Cunningham said decisively. 'We must take a charitable view of it.'
'They say a man who does it is a coward,' Mr Dedalus said. 'It is not for us to judge,' Martin Cunningham said.

The era of scientific research and the objective approach had begun and remains with us to this very day. The severity of Christian condemnation has receded without reducing the appreciation of human life, to whose preservation the medical profession and voluntary bodies are committed. We now know that, if not in all cases, certainly in many, the balance of the mind is disturbed and that depression as a prominent feature has had widespread impact, not least on the law itself.

In England suicide used to rank as a felony and attempted

suicide as a misdemeanour. During the years 1946-55 the number of suicidal attempts known to the police in England and Wales was 44,956, of which 5,794 were brought to trial. All but 347 were found guilty. 308 were sentenced to terms of imprisonment without the option of a fine, the rest were put on probation or fined and, as late as 1955, a sentence of two years' imprisonment was imposed which was varied on appeal to one month's imprisonment. This remarkable state of affairs was changed in 1961 when the Suicide Act abrogated the law whereby it was a crime to commit suicide and, as a result, attempted suicide ceased to be a misdemeanour.[17]

Thus the last vestige of legal coercion was removed and the way left open for a harmonious co-operation between psychiatry, the social services and society on this vital subject. Since most people believe in the intrinsic value of life, we must attempt to gain more precise knowledge regarding a person's self-destructive potential and work towards a more accurate response on the part of the family, friends and society to prevent this by offering meaningful alternatives.

Notes

1. Alvarez, A., (1971), *The Savage God,* Weidenfeld & Nicholson, London
2. Rosen, G., (1971), 'History of the Study of Suicide', *Psychological Medicine,* 1:267
3. Perlin, S., (Ed.), (1972), *A Handbook for the Study of Suicide,* Oxford University Press, New York
4. Rosen, *op. cit.*
5. Rosen, *op. cit.,* Vol. I, p. 271
6. Josephus, (1927), English Translation by H. St. J. Thackeray; Vol. 2, pp. 681-3, Loeb Classical Library, London
7. St. John-Stevas, N., (1961), *Life, Death and the Law,* 'Suicide', pp. 232-61
8. Dante, *The Divine Comedy I: Hell,* Trans. Dorothy L. Sayers, Penguin Books, Harmondsworth; Canto XIII, pp. 150-2
9. Donne, J., (1930), *Biothanatos,* Facsimile Text Society, New York

10. *Ibid.*, p. 18
11. Burton, R., (1927), *The Anatomy of Melancholy,* Tudor Publishing Company, New York, pp. 368-74
12. Hume, D., (1898), *Essays, Moral, Political and Literary,* London, Vol. II, pp. 410-12
13. Cheyne, G., (1733), *The English Malady,* Straham and Locke, London
14. Spurzheim, J. G., (1818), *Observations sur la Folie, ou sur les derangements des functions morales et intellectuelles de l'homme,* Treuttel et Wurtz, Paris, pp. 207-20
15. Esquirol, E., (1838), *Des Maladies mentales considerées sous les Rapports medical, hygienique et medico legal,* 526-676, Bailliere, Paris
16. Alvarez, *op. cit.,* pp. 170-9
17. Stengel, E., (1964), *Suicide and Attempted Suicide,* Pelican, Harmondsworth

XVII Suicide

As a form of regulation of human behaviour the law is increasingly considered to be an unsuitable way of influencing conduct affecting the individual private life. Although suicide is undoubtedly a very private act, the forces which influence it spring as much from the community which surrounds the individual, as from within him.

E. Durkheim's monograph on *Suicide*, published in 1897, set out what has now become a classical formulation of the social factors relating to suicide.[1] Environment, in the form of the values, attitudes, coherence, support, or lack of support, which society offers to the citizen, acts – according to Durkheim – in a positive or negative way in the sustenance of life. A certain amount of suicide was to be expected everywhere but any increase reflected the breakdown of coherence, integration, attachment to or within society. He distinguished three forms of suicide.

The first is called 'Egoistic Suicide' and, as the name suggests, it is the individual who detaches himself from the framework or concern for the society in which he participates. As society has ceased to have any significance for him, the person withdraws into his own system of values.

The second is in some ways exactly the opposite and is called 'Altruistic Suicide' where the person gives up his life for the sake of some exalted, heroic or elevated sense of duty to society. It includes those who give up their lives for others, the elderly who die for the sake of younger people, wives who follow their husbands to the grave, subordinates who die with their master, the ritual hara-kiri of Japanese soldiers and the martyrdom of the early Christians.

The first two refer to the separation of the individual from the community; the third and last form is that of 'Anomic Suicide'. Here it is society which changes, by loosening its standards, or the cohesion and the firmness of control it has over the individual. Clearly at a time like ours when there is unprecedented social, moral, religious and family upheaval with increasing emphasis on individualism, this form has a marked relevance which continues some three-quarters of a century after the inception of this theory.

Durkheim is one of the giants of modern sociology who takes his stand on the importance of social factors in the shaping, direction and control of human behaviour. At about the same time Freud was beginning to construct his theories of the determinants of the human personality which take as their basis the exactly opposite view, namely that human behaviour is the expression of the development of all those psychological influences that occur in the course of the individual's development, particularly the instinct of self-preservation and self-destruction, the Eros-Thanatos polarity. In the psychoanalytic world the person pursues his own individual journey largely influenced by inner instinctual experiences, needs and drives. Aggression played a prominent part in Freudian theory and is neatly summarized in the following sentences:

> The fateful question for the human species seems to me to be whether, and to what extent, their cultural development will succeed in mastering the disturbance of their communal life by the human instinct of aggression and self-destruction. It may be that in this respect precisely that they would have no difficulty in exterminating one another to the last man.[2]

Freud noted man's basic instinct for aggression and suggested that civilization has no future unless this can be controlled effectively at a time when man has such powerful weapons. What was true in 1930 is even more so forty years later.

The wholesale destruction of nations is the final expression of collective aggression; the elimination of an individual through his own voluntary effort was ultimately for Freud aggression turned inward towards the self. This tendency towards self-annihilation can result either from aggression directed at others, turned the other way round towards oneself or from what Freud called a death instinct.

After long hesitancies and vacillation we have decided to assume the existence of only two basic instincts, Eros and the destructive instinct. The aim of the first of these basic instincts is to establish even greater unities and to preserve them – in short to bind together; the aim of the second is, on the contrary, to undo connections and so to destroy things. In the case of the destructive instinct, we may suppose that its final aim is to turn what is living into an inorganic state.[3]

The concept of a death instinct has not found favour amongst psychoanalysts but the expression of aggression towards oneself primarily or secondarily from others, turned backwards towards oneself, is an extensive phenomenon which accounts for much of the emotional background of suicides. Naturally the earliest bonds of love and anger are formed between children and their parents and much aggression results from the feelings generated in this relationship.

The structure of these feelings forms the bulk of the literature of dynamic psychology of the last seventy-five years and only the merest outline will be offered here.

The formation of the original bond between child and parents, between siblings themselves and between children, relatives and friends forms the foundation of all loving relationships, and the earliest human turbulence is the loss of a loved object. We know that this loss leads to an intense sense of misery and depression as well as anger at feeling abandoned.

Apart from loss, there is the constant presence of ambivalence, that is to say those we love have also the capacity to deny, deprive, misunderstand, reject, object to, hurt, humiliate us and so our feelings fluctuate from love to intense hostility. When we hate we may also feel sorry, miserable, guilty; we want not only to punish others for hurting us but also to punish ourselves for our hasty, aggressive response to those we love.

Furthermore, in the course of growth, we depend on parents or parent substitutes for the feelings of being recognized, wanted, appreciated; in other words of being loved. We are thus totally dependent initially on others for our self-esteem and for the image we have of ourselves. There are those who are unfortunate enough to receive consistently negative signals of rejection, insufficient appreciation, a sense of dismissal, unworthiness, and so their feelings about themselves are consistently self-rejecting; this group contributes largely to the amount of suicidal activity.

Thus the sense of feeling lovable, through expressing or receiving love from others, is the basis of self-acceptance, whereas its lack, or the presence of marked feelings of self-rejection, often form the emotional background of destructive suicidal behaviour.

Durkheim and Freud form the two poles of thought on the social and psychological influences which contribute to the loss of life and nowadays it is the interaction between the two that forms the basis of scientific examination of the factors that contribute to suicide.

INCIDENCE

The first responsibility of science is to determine with all possible accuracy the size of a phenomenon; this lifts the debate from the level of rumour and gossip to that of accuracy and reality. This is not to say that the matter ends with the arrival of figures, but it does spare the discussion the embroidery of exaggeration and distortion. Facts about suicide are not easy to amass because of the various ways that a death might be interpreted in the absence of a clear-cut suicidal gesture such as hanging oneself, or throwing oneself in front of a train. Despite these inherent difficulties there do exist international statistics calculated on the basis of deaths per 100,000 of the population.

One feature stands out clearly; namely that men are far more prone to suicide than women, a fact recorded in every

D   G

TABLE V

Deaths by suicide per 100,000 population for the year 1967

	Males	Females
UK	11·4	7·6
Belgium	20·9	9·3
France	23·3	8·0
Germany (Fed. Rep.)	29·5	13·9
Italy	7·8	3·2
Luxembourg	17·6	9·4
Netherlands	7·9	4·5
Denmark	23·6	11·6
Irish Republic	3·7	1·2
Norway	10·6	3·5
Spain	6·7	2·3
Switzerland	26·5	9·1
USA	15·7	6·1
Canada	13·2	4·8
Japan	16·1	12·1

(*Social Trends* 1972: Table 167)

country. In a separate table the rate of death per 100,000 of the population from different causes shows that suicide is the fourth most common cause of death after heart conditions, cancer and motor vehicle accidents.

TABLE VI

Selected Causes of Death per 100,000 population in 1967 of the United Kingdom

All Causes	Infective and Parasitic	Malig- nant	Cardio- Vas- cular Diseases	Suicide	Homi- cide	Motor Vehicle Acci- dents
Male 1,182·4	10·4	253·5	579·8	11·4	0·8	21·2
Female 1,064·4	6·2	201·5	583·2	7·6	7·6	8·9

The collection of accurate information also provides the opportunity to assess whether there is an increase or decrease in suicide rates. The results are not clear cut. Looking at the figures for the thirty years between 1922 and 1953 of countries which have kept records, suicide in men has decreased overall because of the fall in the younger age groups but, in the over-sixties, it has fallen in some countries and increased in others. Suicide in women is, on the other hand, increasing because the rate for those over sixty has risen significantly. Nevertheless the conclusion of Dr Sainsbury, an authority on the subject, is that the profound social changes in Westernized society do not therefore appear to have been consistently harmful to mental well-being, if suicide is the criterion; though elderly women are apparently being increasingly vulnerable to suicide.[4] Women nevertheless commit suicide very much less often than men, despite there being more women in the world.

More specifically, the actual number and rate of suicides in England and Wales are given below.

TABLE VII

	Number of suicides in England & Wales	Rate per 100,000 in England & Wales
1960	5112	11–2
1965	5161	10·8
1970	3939	8·0

There was a considerable drop taking place between 1965 and 1970 and in Chapter XIX the relationship between this and the Samaritans will be discussed.

Another feature that is pretty constant is that suicide rates increase with age. The rate doubles between the second and third decade and in males reaches a peak at about

sixty-five where a peak occurs at about fifty-five in women.[5]
These facts fit closely with the increased evidence of depression in the second half of life.

The relationship between suicide and depression is a close one. It has been estimated that at least 50 per cent of those dying by suicide had a depressive illness at the time of death.[6] This figure is probably too low, for when the home of the suicide was visited soon after the event and relations were asked for detailed information, it was concluded that no less than 94 per cent of the suicides were in need of psychiatric treatment at the time, of which 69 per cent were suffering either from depression or alcoholism.[7]

What contributes to the depressive illness? The answer can be divided into two parts. On the one hand there are those who are particularly prone to the illness itself; on the other hand, there are the rest who have a whole variety of personal stress factors which trigger off a depressive reaction of sufficient intensity to make them wish to terminate life.

Information regarding association between depressive illness and suicide is now extensive. Thus one in six of patients diagnosed as suffering from a manic-depressive illness can be expected to take their own life[8] and this risk is four times greater in men than in women.[9] This high risk for those suffering from depressive illness has also a critical time in that the six month period following discharge from hospital is the most dangerous time for suicide.[10]

So far the link between suicide and depression has been shown to include both sexes in the older age group, but for men in particular – and especially if they have been treated for a depressive illness – the first six months after discharge is particularly dangerous. Three other features are also commonly associated. Such a person will frequently live alone, have suffered the loss of the spouse and be drinking heavily.

These are the negative elements. Are there any protective, positive elements apart from freedom from the depressive illness? Generally speaking the advantages lie with being a woman, and, for both sexes, young, married, believing in a faith which condemns suicide and – ironically – living in a country which is in a state of war! Suicide rates fall during wartime. In every belligerent country during World War II there was a marked decrease in suicide. This decrease fits in beautifully with Freud's theories whereby the collective aggressiveness of a country is directed outwardly towards a common enemy. But it also fits in with Durkheim's view that war conditions bring about a much greater cohesion, integration and sharing of values so that war brings about a 'common conscience' in the country. The figures in Table I also show a particularly low rate in traditionally Roman Catholic countries such as Italy, Eire and Spain.

All these are large-scale statistical data. Is there any more direct information, more clues of the interaction on suicide from the subjects who actively commit it? One way of gathering this information is from analysing suicide notes (left by about 15 per cent of those who succeed in their attempt) and some 568 were so analysed.[11]

In some 81 per cent of the notes, there was evidence of frustrated desire which took three forms; the first is personal – 'I have been in ill health since last May, there is no hope.' 'I can't hear.' 'I'm too lonely.' 'I don't have a friend.' The second is frustration arising from others – 'I hope nobody hurts you like you have me.' 'I have been treated like a dog.' 'Mother has made a sucker out of me.' 'I cannot live without Dad.' 'I can never stop loving you so I shall take this way out.' The third is an internal frustration – 'I am such an anxiety and burden to you.' 'You have all tried everything to help me be myself again but it's no use.'

In some 59 per cent of notes a person seems to reach an intolerable level of strain: 'I am all mixed up.' 'I'm lost and frightened.' 'I can't stand no more.' 'I can't go on like this.' In 17 per cent the persons actively dislike themselves: 'I have been a sham and a fake.' 'I've always been a misfit.' 'This is the only decent thing to do.' In 6 per cent of the statements, the suicides believed that they were expected to act in this way: 'This is what you wanted.' 'I took the pills for you.' 'I hope you are satisfied.' And in another 6 per cent the feeling becomes more accusatory: 'You drove me to this.' 'You have killed me.' In 4 per cent the aggressive, punitive element is clear: 'I hope you have my last breath on your mind for ever.' 'I hope each time you pass a cemetery you will have memories of one who is there.'

In no less than 38 per cent of the notes the idea of suicide has been present for some time: 'I have wanted it for a long time.' 'I have put it off as long as I can.' These notes are in keeping with the statistical data that those who attempt suicide and are unsuccessful are more inclined to try again. It is simply not true that those who were unsuccessful have learned their lesson.

Perhaps part of this insistence lies in the conviction found in 7 per cent of the notes which suggests that the frustration experienced in this life might somehow be made up after death: 'I believe we will meet later under favourable circumstances.' 'I hope one day we will meet in heaven.' 'I am going to meet my Dad.' 'I will be released in the kingdom.'

It can easily be seen that all these notes are associated with intense misery and sadness, both prominent features of depression and brought about by a variety of intra- and interpersonal conflict.

In a recent study[12] the motives of 79 graduate students from the University of Illinois, USA, were analysed. Their average age was 24.2 years and the sample consisted of 43 who were planning and had secured the means to commit suicide, 21 who had sought help for their suicidal thoughts and actions and 15 who had attempted suicide.

The analysis of the replies indicated that these men and women could be divided into four groups. The first and largest group had a high incidence of loneliness, loss of someone close, sexual problems and the break-up of an important relationship. The second had marked health problems: the third felt acutely the fear of failure and the future looked dim: and the fourth showed the distinct desire to hurt or manipulate another person.

What emerges from studies of suicide is that, when all the information we have about it at present is examined, it leads to the problem frequently discussed in this book. Depression is an illness. Depression also becomes an illness

springing from intolerable personal stress. Depression is a
reaction to stress, even though it may not assume all the
characteristics of illness. Intimately connected with all forms
of depression is the gloom that seeks ultimately to put an
end to suffering. For some the suffering ends when the
illness is relieved; for others the stress is reversible or
manageable; for others the stress is neither reversible nor
negotiable. All suffer from depression but for some it is an
illness with an intact past and anticipatory joyful future;
for others the lifting of the depression leaves the wounds
and scars of the past as a continuing contribution to the
fragility of the future.

Statistics can certainly point the way to prevention and
this will be considered in Chapter XIX, but we need an artist
to sum up the inner world of the would-be suicide in a
description that goes beyond statistics, into a psychology
of global feelings. Boris Pasternak wrote about the Russian
poets who had begun their work before 1917 and refused to
compromise themselves after the Revolution. In writing
about them, he is also saying something of a universal quality
about all those who enter this extraordinary lonely journey.
Here the circle has been completed and the attitude of St
Augustine that suicide was a cowardly act has given way
to an understanding of the immense suffering that precedes
the attempt or the successful act which has little to do with
cowardice and a great deal more with desperation – the
desperation of failing to understand or be understood, the
inability to reach or be reached, accept or be accepted,
receive or be received, communicate or be communicated
with, feel free, ultimately feel meaningful to oneself and/or
others.

To start with what is most important: we have no conception of the inner torture which precedes suicide.
People who are physically tortured on the rack keep
losing consciousness, their suffering is so great that its
unendurable intensity shortens the end. But a man who
is thus at the mercy of the executioner is not annihilated
when he faints from pain, for he is present at his own
end, his past belongs to him, his memories are his and,

if he chooses, he can make use of them, they can help him before his death.

But a man who decides to commit suicide puts a full stop to his being, he turns his back on his past, he declares himself a bankrupt and his memories to be unreal. They can no longer help or save him, he has put himself beyond their reach. The continuity of his inner life is broken, his personality is at an end. And perhaps what finally makes him kill himself is not the firmness of his resolve but the unbearable quality of this anguish which belongs to no one, of this suffering in the absence of the sufferer, of this waiting which is empty because life has stopped and can no longer fill it.

It seems to me that Mayakovsky shot himself out of pride, because he condemned something in himself, or close to him, to which his self-respect could not submit. That Yesenin hanged himself without having properly thought out the consequences of his act, still saying in his inmost heart: 'Who knows? Perhaps this isn't yet the end. Nothing is yet decided.' That Maria Tsvetayeva had always held her work between herself and the reality of daily life; and when she found this luxury beyond her means, when she felt that for her son's sake she must, for a time, give up her passionate absorption in poetry and look round her soberly, she saw chaos. No longer screened by art, fixed, unfamiliar, motionless, and, not knowing where to run for terror, she hid in death, putting her head into the noose as she might have hidden her head under her pillow. It seems to me that Paolo Yashvili was utterly confused, spellbound by the Shigalyovshchina of 1937 as by witchcraft; and that he watched his daughter as she slept at night and, imagining himself unworthy to look at her, went out in the morning to his friends' house and blasted his head with grapeshot from his double-barrelled gun. And it seemed to me that Fadeyev, still with the apologetic smile which had somehow stayed with him through all the crafty ins and outs of politics, told himself just before he pulled the trigger: 'Well, now it's over. Goodbye, Sasha.'

What is certain is that they all suffered beyond description, to the point where suffering has become a mental sickness. And, as we bow in homage to their gifts and to their bright memory, we should bow compassionately before their suffering.[18]

Notes

1. Durkheim, E., (1952), *Suicide* (Trans.), Routledge and Kegan Paul, London
2. Freud, S., (1930), *Civilization and its Discontents; Works,* Hogarth Press, London, Vol. XXI, p. 145
3. Freud, S., (1940), *An Outline of Psychoanalysis; Works,* Hogarth Press, London, Vol. XXIII, p. 148
4. Sainsbury, P., (1968), *Suicide and Depression in Recent Developments in Affective Disorders,* R.M.P.A.
5. *Ibid.*
6. Barraclough, B. M., Nelson, B., Burch, J., Sainsbury, P., (1970), *Proceedings of the Fifth Conference of Suicide Prevention,* Vienna
7. Robins, E., *et al,* (1959), 'Some clinical considerations in the Prevention of Suicide based on a study of 134 successful suicides', *American Journal of Public Health,* 49:888
8. Sainsbury, *op. cit.,* p. 1
9. Pitts, F. N., Winokor, G., (1964), 'Affective disorder III: diagnostic correlations and incidence of suicide', *Journal of Nervous Disorder,* 139, 176
10. Sainsbury, *op. cit.,* p. 11
11. Bjerg Kresten, (1967), 'The Suicidal Life Space—attempts at a reconstruction from suicide notes' in *Essays in self-destruction,* Science House
12. Colson, C., (1973), 'An Objective-Analytic Approach to the classification of Suicide Intervention Act', *Acta Psychiatrica Scandinavica,* 49, 105
13. Pasternak, B., (1959), *An Essay in Autobiography,* trans. Manya Harari, Collins, London and New York, pp. 91-3

XVIII   Attempted Suicide

The previous chapter described those whose suicide attempts were successful. If a person leaves a note behind saying that he wanted to kill himself, there can be no argument about his intention. However, it is unlikely that everybody who attempts suicide actually wishes to die. The discussion of what criteria should be adopted to differentiate and define the range of intent occupies millions of words in professional literature and its examination here would take us a long way from the subject of depression.

There are certain factors, however, which are incontrovertible. Although the figures of those who actually succeed and those who do not certainly overlap, there are a number of characteristics that differentiate the two which we will briefly consider.

INCIDENCE OF ATTEMPTED SUICIDE

As in the case of successful suicide, the size of the problem is the first consideration. If details of actual suicide are restricted, those of attempted suicide are even more so, particularly when, as until recently, it was a matter of infringing the law. Such studies as do exist put the ratio of attempted suicide to actual suicide between 10 and 20 to 1. What is more, unlike the numbers of actual suicides, attempted suicides are very much on the increase.

AGE AND SEX

Not only are attempted suicides far more frequent but they involve a different age group and sex distribution. As the graph below shows, the age is much earlier than actual suicides and there is a preponderance of females.

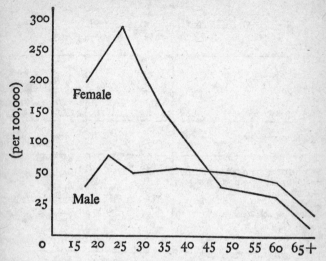

Figure 2. Self-poisoning: one year rates per
100,000 by age and sex; Edinburgh adults only.

THE SETTING OF THE SUICIDE ATTEMPT

One way of comparing the firmness of intent as between
those who unequivocally want to kill themselves and those
who do not is to look for the possibility of intervention at
the time of the act.

Table VIII shows that successful suicides were usually
much further from the possibility of being reached. In particular, those who were alone formed nearly 52 per cent of
those who committed suicide, compared to 26 per cent of
those who were unsuccessful.

Those who have no ultimate intention of committing
suicide tend on the whole to make their attempt in a place
where they are liable to be discovered or are near enough
to people who could intervene or who might come soon, or
interrupt their procedure by making their act known in

TABLE VIII

Degree of Isolation during suicidal Act
(*Figures in brackets are the number of patients*)

| | Group A2 Attempted Suicides | | Group B Suicides | |
	Men (66)	Women (101)	Men (73)	Women (44)
Special person near	11	16	16	5
Special person no relevant data	2	2	—	—
Special person in company	5	4	—	—
Others near	20	32	26	8
Others in company	6	4	—	—
Others no relevant data	—	4	—	—
Alone	14	30	30	31
Unknown	8	9	1	—

time. All these precautions mitigate the chances of death but do not completely eliminate it. Sometimes the gamble does not come off: people die by mistake.

Another factor frequently associated with the attempted suicide is its impulsive nature. In an extensive study of self-poisoning, it was found that two-thirds of all acts were impulsive, and here is how the author of the study describes this:

This astonishing finding is of the utmost importance. Five minutes, sometimes only one minute, before the act took place the idea of taking poison was not in the person's mind. He may have, he often had, thought about it in the past. Hours of rumination may have preceded the determination which was formed in a single moment. But in the event, at the event, a feeling of despair arose, often suddenly, from a trivial cause, and was as suddenly acted upon. It was no culmination of a gathering plan. 'Why did you do it?' the patients are asked. 'I don't know; it just came over me,' they reply. They are not prevaricat-

ing. They never worked it out. They never had a period
when they were intending to do it. It just came over
them.[1]

The connection with depression remains but it is not
so marked as in the case of suicide, which is only to be
expected considering the age group involved. These are
younger men and women with much less chance of being
severely depressed but who are much more likely to be
depressed as a reaction to a particularly distressing life
situation. This reaction is somewhere between being distressed
and actively depressed, with a much greater preponderance
of what has been described as a reactive depression.

In the age group under consideration, we would expect
to find suicidal attempts arising out of the life situations which
are universally present in this phase in life. Thus, the
adolescent will swallow a handful of tablets to show his
frustration against authoritarian parents, to express the despair
of feeling unloved, of anger over real or imagined favouritism
of parents towards a sister or brother, of disappointment
at having failed to please parents over exams, of feeling ugly,
unattractive and socially isolated, after rejection by a boy-
friend or girl-friend, failure at work or of being unable to
leave home and lead a separate life.

Suicidal attempts are extremely common in marriages
under tension, and in the study quoted, marital disharmony
forms the major precipitating factor. The spouse who is
actively rejected in favour of another man or woman, who
is desperately keen to retain their partner's affection, who
is lonely after being deserted, who is drinking to drown the
grief of abandonment, who cannot live with his or her
spouse and yet cannot live without them, who feels a failure
and responsible for the breakdown, who is furious with
their adulterous, alcoholic or persecuting husband or wife,
all of these can react via attempted suicide.

Separation from home, heterosexual relationships, marriage, work, money, housing are the challenges of the first
half of life and it is the inability to cope that leads to the
type of distress that can provoke attempted suicide.

If the ultimate aim of such an attempt is not death then

what is it? The simplest reply is that the attempted suicide is a cry for help. Through it, attention is attracted when the person no longer knows what to think, say or do which will be effective. Parents, spouse, relatives and friends suddenly see their desperation and are moved in a way they would not have been before. It is a final act of giving up but not of terminating life. There is acute distress but the will to live has not been extinguished. The social isolation is broken. Admission to hospital, attention from doctors, nurses, social workers and the family, may bring respite and, what is more, someone yields, someone concedes a point, someone takes fresh cognizance of the situation, someone responds. For many the crisis has brought a new lease of life. But not for everybody.

In one study 204 patients who had made a suicidal attempt were followed up for two years in which it was found that 26 per cent had made a further attempt and 2 per cent had killed themselves. Five factors were identified which in combination successfully predicted 80 per cent of those who repeated their suicidal attempts.[2] These factors were (a) antisocial personality, (b) organic brain disorder, (c) a previous attempt, (d) widowhood, separation or divorce, (e) membership of the Registrar General Classification I to III.

One element that stands out in these findings is the likelihood that the person who is making repeated suicidal attempts finds it very difficult to cope with life either alone or in relationship with others. Recently attention has been drawn to the cycle of human deprivation. Children brought up in adverse circumstances may suffer from certain personality defects as a consequence. They grow up and repeat the same defective pattern in their later life, in turn affecting their children.

We would expect the case histories of suicidal attempts to show some evidence of a disrupted home life and, indeed, the evidence is overwhelmingly present. If parental disruption is interpreted to mean parental death, desertion, conflict between or divorce of parents, then all but two of fourteen studies carried out in several parts of the world show a presence of disruption well above that to be found in the population generally.

Thus the suicidal attempt sets the seal on a life-pattern characterized by adverse circumstances – a bad work record, chronic debt, constant changes of home, often the product of separations . . . which seemed to repeat a similar story in the parents.

A suicide attempt springs from a situation characterized by despair, depression and doubt, summed up here by a woman of thirty who took a handful of the tranquillizers with which her depression was being treated.

I took them because I could not go on. I wanted Jim back. He left me a week ago. He has been playing about with another woman. If my marriage breaks up, it will be the same as my own home. Ever since I remember as a child my father played about with women. My mother took it. I swore no man would do that to me. I am furious and it hurts but there is also something wrong with me. Jim is not like my father. I said just now he was playing around with another woman. That's not true. I pushed him into it. I told him if he didn't like it, he could look for somebody else and he did. I got what I asked. Now I want nothing except him. Without him life is nothing. I can't face my mother; I can't live on my own; I can't cope. I did not want to kill myself, just to get him back. It's blackmail I know, but if it doesn't succeed . . . the next time . . . there won't be a second chance, I will make damn sure.

Notes

1. Kessel, N., (1965), 'Self-Poisoning', *British Medical Journal*, 2; 1336
2. Bagley, C., Greer, S., (1971), 'Clinical and Social predictions of repeated attempted suicide', *British Journal of Psychiatry*, 119, 515

XIX Outlook and Prevention of Depression and Suicide

The woman anxious to be reconciled with her husband could see no prospect of a happy life unless he returned. In fact, a good deal more than his return would be required. There would have to be some sort of reconstruction in their relationship which would meet their minimum physical, emotional and social needs. But no reconstruction could take place until the emergency brought about by the crisis was resolved.

In dealing with the outlook of those who find themselves in a state of despair and depression, we must divide the problems into those arising from the clear-cut presence of depressive illness ('endogenous' or 'reactive') and those arising from the solution of the life crisis – if any – which triggered off these depressive reactions. The most accurate information exists in the prognosis of manic depressive illness itself.

PROGNOSIS OF MANIC-DEPRESSIVE ILLNESS

Writing at the beginning of the seventeenth century, Robert Burton in his *Anatomy of Melancholy* had this to say about its prognosis:

> And both men and women must take notice of that saying of Montanus: this malady doth commonly accompany them to their grave: Physicians may ease, and it may lie hid for a time, but they cannot quite cure it, but it will return again more violent and sharp than at first . . . Seldom this malady procures death, except (which is the greatest most grievous calamity, and the misery of all miseries) they make away with themselves, which is a frequent thing and familiar amongst them.[1]

Burton has recognized the seriousness of the depressive illness, its tendency to recur and the risk of suicide, all of which remain correct assessments of the serious, 'endogenous' form of depressive illness.

The author of an extensive study[2] published in 1945 which included the severe forms of depressive and manic illness, reached the following conclusions (the period of examination concerned the days before effective therapy in the absence of ECT).

The prognosis for complete recovery from the first attack is very good. 80 per cent of all depressives recover and 92 per cent of all sufferers from manic illness. The duration of both illnesses for those under the age of thirty is usually six to nine months, while for those over thirty the duration is nearly twice the length.

The risk of recurrence for depression is less than for mania. Two-thirds of all the depressive cases had only a single attack, but only half of the patients with manic illnesses had only a single attack.

If a patient has a second attack, the prognosis for recovery is also high, about 85 per cent. The risk of multiple attacks is greater for manic and for older age depressives.

With the advent of electroconvulsive therapy, the single greatest advance has been the reduction of the duration of the illness from six to nine months to a third of that interval or less, except in the severest cases. These remain, and are seen in hospital admissions.

In a more recent survey[3] of 100 admissions between 1947 and 1949, 50 spent more than 4 months, and 9 patients at least 4.5 years in hospital. Of 100 discharges, 40 were readmitted at least once during the subsequent 4 years, of whom another 20 were readmitted at least once more during the same period. The crude death rate during the first year of hospital life was 121/1000 for men (three times the expected rate for males over fifty) and 77/1000 for females (more than twice the expected rate for females over fifty).

The era of these studies coincided with the arrival of ECT but preceded the availability of antidepressants. At that stage the prognosis for the individual attack had vastly improved in terms of period of hospitalization, although it still remained a serious disease.

Finally, since the middle of the 1950s, antidepressant drugs have been widely used and the ultimate significance of this in terms of prognosis has yet to be fully evaluated. But there are some general remarks that can certainly be made. Some patients who would have previously needed hospitalization are now managed at home, and some patients who would have had to be treated in the outpatient departments of hospitals are now treated successfully by their own family doctor.

In fact, this means that patients treated in hospitals are likely to be suffering from the most severe and intractable of all the depressive illnesses. When this is combined with a study of the older age group, who have a poorer prognosis, then a study[4] published in 1972 gives evidence of sustained positive prognosis with further improvements, although not in any striking manner (not surprising considering the severity of the illness in the hospital group).

Two groups of patients were studied, both over the age of sixty, one treated and followed up in 1950, the other in 1966 (after the introduction of antidepressants). In the 1950 group, 77.7 per cent remained in hospital for more than 3 months as against 41.0 per cent in 1966. Those who did not recover, and remained continuously ill, also showed some improvement in that there were 17.4 per cent in 1950 and only 11.9 per cent in 1966. Suicide, however, remains a risk, one suicide recorded in the earlier and three in the latter group out of eighty-one and ninety-two patients respectively.

To sum up, the presence of ECT and antidepressant drugs can rapidly cut short the overwhelming majority of severe depressions so that long periods of illness are now extremely rare. But in a few people recurrence remains a problem. Here there is now a further ray of hope in the expanding use of the drug lithium, which studies are beginning to show can undoubtedly reduce the recurrence rate for manic and depressive illnesses. In one investigation[5] patients who had more than three attacks of depression were followed up for at least $2\frac{1}{4}$ years. Those who were not treated with lithium spent 30 per cent of their time with further depressive illness despite all forms of treatment, whereas those treated with lithium had this time reduced to 5 per cent. Another more recent study confirms this opinion.[6]

It is not too presumptuous, therefore, to expect that in the very near future most, if not all, forms of severe depressive illness will be capable of reversal provided that there are no complications arising from the sufferer's personality or life situation and which therefore perpetuate the condition. (It should be added that this rate of recovery has yet to be reached. There are still a few intractable depressions although the number is minute.) All this assumes that the person has the type of depression which responds to treatment or that the person actually finds their way to their doctor. There are those for whom these conditions do not prevail. They are in desperate need of help with their depression but they cannot bring themselves to visit a doctor or, if they can, he gives them insufficient help.

These people are those with personal difficulties that appear to them embarrassing and humiliating. They may be in trouble with the law; they may be in financial difficulties; perhaps their marriage is in distress and they see no way out, they suffer from sexual difficulties often called deviations, they are in conflict with their parents, they are lonely, isolated, have no relatives, no one to turn to, are extremely frightened and sensitive, are using excesses of alcohol or drugs in fruitless attempts to relieve their gloom; they may be acutely mentally ill with a primary depressive illness or other conditions. They all reach a moment of despair and they want to finish it all.

SAMARITANS

A clergyman called Chad Varah felt that there should be some way of helping these people. And so the Samaritans began their work in 1953. It is a movement which has grown from an originally unrecorded number of clients who made use of the Samaritans to 12,355 in 1964, rising to 156,722 in 1972.

These clients are all listened to over the telephone and, whenever possible, invited to come to the centre or are personally befriended for the crisis period. If necessary they are encouraged to receive medical help. The twenty principles of the Samaritans are printed below and make it absolutely clear that a caller will at all times be treated with total respect, be absolutely sure that their information will be treated in complete confidence and that the Samaritan will do his utmost to share and respond with care to their suffering.

Twenty Principles of the Samaritans[7]

Originally formulated and revised by Chad Varah. Further revised by him at the request of the Council of Management, and approved by its Executive Committee on 10 January 1973.

1. The Samaritans are a world-wide fellowship of volunteers dedicated to the prevention of suicide and the alleviation of the loneliness and depression that may lead to it, by making their befriending immediately available at any hour of the day or night to those who feel they have no one else to turn to in their distress.

2. The befriending which the volunteer offers to the caller is the personal concern of a compassionate fellow human being who, like the Samaritan in the parable, seeks simply to love him as a friend in his time of deepest need.

3. The volunteers are carefully selected for their personal qualities and natural aptitude for the work, without regard to their creed, colour, politics, age, sex or status.

4. The volunteers in each Centre recognized as a Branch of The Samaritans work under the supervision of a Director (or Chairman) and other Leaders, who are

advised by Consultants with medical or other professional qualifications, so that the highest standards of caring may be achieved. Consultants may also assist in the selection and preparation of volunteers and give help to clients.

5. In countries where the telephone is generally available, an easily remembered telephone number is advertised by each Branch, in addition to its address, to enable swift (and, if the caller desires, anonymous) contact to be made with the minimum effort on the part of the caller.

6. The Samaritans receive callers in person at their Centre, and invite telephone callers who seem likely to benefit to meet a Samaritan face to face. Callers are free if they wish to have contact only by telephone or by letter.

7. The Samaritans' primary and overriding concern is for those who seem to be in immediate danger of taking their own lives.

8. Samaritans engage in long-term as well as short-term prevention of suicide by befriending despairing and lonely people who do not seem to be suicidal at the time when they seek help, or who seem unlikely for conscientious or other reasons ever to commit suicide.

9. If a caller is concerned about another person, the Samaritans try to support him in his anxiety and to suggest ways of obtaining help for his friend. The Samaritans do not intrude upon persons who have not sought their help directly, unless an identified responsible person informs them of the need of someone who is too young or old or ill to ask in person, in which case they may make a tentative offer of help.

10. The Samaritans do not permit their immediate availability in cases of a suicidal emergency to be impeded by attention to cases of long-term chronic inadequacy,

though callers in this category may be accepted as clients during a crisis.

11. The Samaritans do not flatter themselves that what they have to offer will be helpful to every caller. Those in charge of each Branch are responsible for using their human resources to the best advantage, and protecting them from being wasted by the grossly psychopathic or any others not capable of benefiting from befriending.

12. The Samaritans' service is non-medical. Callers requesting medical treatment may be helped to obtain this, and each Branch has at least one medical consultant, usually a psychiatrist, to advise those in charge of the Branch about such cases.

13. The Samaritans are not a trained case-work agency, and volunteers are not permitted to attempt to do for a client in an amateur way what social workers are trained to do with professional competence.

14. The Samaritans are not a social welfare agency. They refer those who request material aid to the appropriate welfare service, except in countries which lack these.

15. The Samaritans are not a Christian organization, except in the origin of the concept. Volunteers, whatever their original beliefs, are strictly forbidden to make any attempt to convert the callers or to exploit a caller's distress by using the opportunity to witness to the volunteer's beliefs. Callers spontaneously requesting spiritual help of a particular kind are referred, with their permission, to a representative of the appropriate body, who may or may not be a member of the organization.

16. Volunteers are normally known to callers only by their Christian names or forenames and their volunteer's identification number, unless continued befriending by

a chosen volunteer is arranged, when one of the persons in charge of the Branch decides what other information may be given to the client concerned and whether hospitality may be offered by the volunteer in his or her home.

17. The fact that a person has sought the help of The Samaritans, and everything he has confided in them, is confidential within the organization. All communications from callers which could reasonably be regarded as of a highly secret nature, and those relating to criminal acts, are received in the strictest confidence and are revealed neither to any person outside the organization without the caller's express permission, nor to persons within the organization who are not involved, except the Director. Volunteers are not permitted to accept confidences if a condition is made that not even the Director should be informed of them.

18. The caller remains at all times in charge of his own destiny and is free to reject the help that is offered and to break contact without fear of being sought out against his will, even if it is felt certain that he intends to take his own life or to commit some other act which The Samaritans would deprecate. A volunteer in contact (whether by telephone or face to face) with a caller judged to be in some danger of suicide is encouraged to seek the caller's permission for a discreet approach to be made to him subsequently to ask how he is, and to record the fact if permission is granted. In such cases 'follow up' is clearly not against the client's will.

19. The various Branches of The Samaritans are banded together in a legally constituted Association whose Council of Management represents all the Branches and reserves to itself the appointment of the person in charge of each Branch, responsible for seeing that the above-mentioned principles are observed.

20. Only the Council may authorize departures from these
    principles, for instance by permitting new Branches
    to offer a limited service for a period, or overseas
    Branches to use some other name; and only the Council
    may from time to time revise these principles.

A chance to be listened to, welcomed and have your cares
shared eases the distress. Does it actually save lives? Dr
R. Fox presented a table which is reproduced below, drawing attention to the relationship between the decline of
suicides, the rise in Samaritan branches and the number of
new clients.[8] This could be a coincidence but there is strong
suggestion that it is not.

TABLE IX

	Population in millions England and Wales	Number of suicides England and Wales	Rate per 100,000 England and Wales	Samaritan Branches in UK on 31 Dec.	Number of new clients	Number of Volunteers
1959	43·39	5,207	11·5	2	Not recorded	Not recorded
1960	45·76	5,112	11·2	7	,, ,,	,, ,,
1961	46·17	5,200	11·3	17	,, ,,	,, ,,
1962	46·67	5,588	12·0	28	,, ,,	,, ,,
1963	47·02	5,714	12·2	41	,, ,,	,, ,,
1964	47·40	5,566	11·7	56	12,355	,, ,,
1965	47·76	5,161	10·8	68	16,422	6,537
1966	49·08	4,994	10·4	75	20,875	7,116
1967	48·39	4,711	9·7	86	31,780	7,688
1978	48·67	4,584	9·4	92	42,241	11,204
1969	48·83	4,370	8·9	95	51,412	8,910
1970	48·94	3,939	8·0	115	68,531	12,832
1971	48·81	3,945	8·08	122	89,254	15,225
1972*		3,819		132	156,722	15 729

Drop: 1963-71 = 34%

*Estimated first six months, 1939; first nine months, 2,864

There are, of course, those whose difficulty arises not from a particular crisis but from a series of crises, because their life is lived in this way. The Samaritans do not aim to give life-long support but neither do they easily reject anyone.

LONG-TERM PREVENTION

Finally, something should be said about the long-term prevention of depression. If the presence of depression was simply the manifestation of a genetic tendency, then short of genetic manipulation or physical therapy, little could be done to avoid it. But this is not the case. The environment, in the form of upbringing and the stability of the home, certainly play a part in the long-term approach to depression.

The interaction between children and parents is one of the most complex processes that human beings negotiate. The child forms a bond with its parents, the severance of which causes a depressive reaction unless adequate and effective surrogate figures take over the task of parental care. The departure of parents, either through death, marital breakdown or for other reasons, is capable of sensitizing the child to the sense of loss and abandonment, both of which evoke a depressive response. If the change of caring figures is frequent, not only is there a repeated formation and disruption of bonds but the growing person learns to expect that 'normality' consists of being let down. Furthermore, in the early years of life the reasons for parental loss or the departure of the parents are not clearly understood and the feeling of personal responsibility, that somehow it was the child's fault, may become part of its guilty attitudes to life. Although the presence of parents establishes a closeness with both, the girl identifies usually with her mother and learns the basis of heterosexual encounter with her father and vice-versa for the boy. Beyond bond formation and the development of sexual identity, the relationship with the parents gives the child the sense of recognition, acceptance and appreciation which collectively give the growing person the sense of personal value, their self-esteem. This may be distorted, of course, without physical absence: both parents may be present but one or both may be unable to show approval or express feelings of appreciation and may even positively show rejection or preference for another child. Here the lack of acceptance is created not by physical absence but by psychological default.

Whatever the reason, children growing up in such adverse environments may reach adulthood with a series of unhappy experiences which singly or together may amount to an absence of the ability to get close to people in general or to the opposite sex, resulting in the feeling that they are lacking in value or significance. Lacking in confidence as a person, in their sexual identity as a man or woman, and therefore generally feeling inadequate, such a person is extremely vulnerable to any form of criticism, rejection or the loss of anything or anyone who is precious to them. They respond to rejection or loss with marked feelings of hurt which is often accompanied with a depressive reaction.

A survey of several studies in 1971 showed that the frequency of parental death during childhood is significantly higher than in matched controls among inpatients (i.e. psychiatric), depressive and alcoholic populations. Also that the frequency of parental separation during childhood is significantly higher in suicidal, personality disorder and schizophrenic populations. The author added from his own investigation the finding that maternal death occurs more commonly in the childhood of the patients suffering from mania and depression than among other types of inpatients.[9]

The exact relationship between such parental disruption and the later development of depression is far from clear, but evidence is beginning to emerge that a relationship does exist and the intactness of the parent-child relationship acts as a form of protection against the later development of severe depressive reactions. We need to know much more about this but that such a relationship should exist is not surprising considering the extended period of human dependence on the parents.

It is unlikely, however, that effectively preventive measures will be speedily applied to this particular contributing factor and so, for the time being, prevention will continue to be a matter of effective therapy and compassionate intervention at times of crisis.

Notes

1. Burton, Robert, *The Anatomy of Melancholy*, Tudor Publishing Co., New York, Part I, Sect. 4; Number I, p. 367
2. Lundquist, G., (1945), *Acta Psychiatrica Neurologica Scandinavica*, Supplement 35
3. Norris, V., (1959), 'Mental illness in London', *Maudsley Monographs*, No. 6, London
4. Post, F., (1972), 'The management and nature of Depressive Illness in Later life, A follow-through study', *British Journal of Psychiatry*, 121, 393
5. Coppen, A. J., *et al.*, (1971), *Lancet*, II, 275
6. Hullin, R. P., *et al.*, (1972), *Lancet*, I, 1044
7. Chad Varah, (1973), *The Samaritans in the 70s*, Constable, pp. 82-6
8. Fox, R., (1971), *Samaritan Contribution to suicide prevention*
9. Atkin, E. D., (1971), 'Parental Deprivation', *Acta Psychiatrica Scandinavica*, Supplement 223

Index